Thailand Redlight

Bangkok: Paradise & Sin

A travel report by

Ted Schneider

Book

Bangkok, a city full of contrasts, is perceived as loud, hectic and disreputable. Despite this, it is one of the most popular cities in the world.

In this report, the protagonist visits many sights and places in Bangkok, Ayutthaya and Kanchanaburi.

In addition, it leads him to the sinful nightlife. Sukhumvit Road is the centre with its hotspots Nana and Soi Cowboy, which lead the protagonist into some erotic adventures.

Finally, he falls in love with an exotic beauty and is confronted with the notorious love disease, leading him into a dangerous emotional chaos.

Author

Ted Schneider was born and raised in Berlin in 1970. Since 2008 he has spent a large part of his life in Indochina, most of the time in Thailand.

Ted Schneider

Thailand Redlight
Bangkok: Paradise & Sin

© 2020 Ted Schneider

1. Edition

E-Mail: t.s.bookinfo@gmail.com

Production and publishing: BoD – Books on Demand, Norderstedt

ISBN: 9783758307430

Prologue

This trip led me to Bangkok. From there I did a small tour to Ayutthaya and Kanchanaburi before I returned to Bangkok.

During the day I went sightseeing and in the evening, I threw myself into the nightlife. On the one hand I was interested in the country and its culture, but on the other hand I was also addicted to the exotic beauties.

The report is based on authentic experiences, condensed to provide maximum information. This has made it possible to describe information about places and sights, accompanied by a story that is not experienced every day.

Besides the sights, I have described the means of transport I used to travel; but my experiences with women are not neglected either, from massages over short sex adventures up to the famous love disease.

The names of the girls have been changed. I have also changed distinctive personality traits in order to exclude any traceability to individuals.

This report was written before the Corona pandemic. Some of the places described may have changed. Some places will have disappeared altogether. However, the story in this report is independent of time and place, as something like this can happen anywhere in Thailand.

1

At 1:45 pm, the Thai Airways plane landed at Suvarnabhumi Airport in Bangkok. Heart pounding, I looked out the window at the temple roofs, the palm trees and the brown water of the rivers. Now the plane had landed and I wondered what was in store for me on this trip. I was sure I would not be disappointed, as this country had so often exceeded my wildest expectations.

Booking the flight went smoothly. My patience had paid off and I got a good price in the high season for under €600. December to March is the best time to travel to Thailand, but also the most expensive.

When booking, I used Kayak and Swoodoo - I always tried out different portals - to find the cheapest airlines and flight times. This time, Thai Airways was one of the cheapest airlines. I booked directly on the Thai Airways website, where the flight was only a few euros more expensive.

I enjoyed the walk through the large, light-flooded corridors of the airport. I was surrounded by a semicircle of steel and glass, with a view of the blue sky. Although the temperature inside the airport was pleasantly cool, I could already sense the tropical heat that awaited me outside.

Airport Suvarnabhumi

I had already filled out the TM30 form during the flight and put it in my passport so I didn't have to look for it at customs.

Arriving at the customs checkpoint, I dutifully got in line and followed the instructions of the staff, who navigated the tourists with hand signals. Although it was a huge queue, everything went quite quickly. The customs officer didn't give me the warmest of welcomes, but that wasn't his job. I followed the instructions by leaving my fingerprints, looking into the gooseneck camera and shutting my face. The customs officer kept the arrival part of the TM30 form, the departure part he gave me back with my passport. I left the snippet in my passport, where it remained until departure.

After collecting my suitcase from the conveyor belt, I arranged for a SIM card for my mobile phone. As usual, I chose dtac, more out of habit than conviction. When I stepped out of the arrival's hall, there were already all the phone provider booths in the long corridor. I passed the providers AIS and True, of which I had never heard anything negative either, and quickly found my provider. The price of about 20 € for a month's phone and internet was OK for me.

Then I followed the "Airport Rail Link" signs all the way down. When I arrived at the ticket machines, I first walked past them and changed money, as the exchange offices in this area have very fair rates.

I bought a ticket from the Airport Rail Link ticket machine to Phaya Thai, the terminus, from where I could continue my journey on the BTS Skytrain. After boarding, I sat on the right side of the train, facing the direction of travel, so that I could admire the skyline on the left.

On previous trips I often took a taxi into town, which has become very easy in Bangkok. I followed the "Public Taxi" signs to get to the taxi area. There, a machine spit out a piece of paper that assigned me a taxi.

I usually went to Pattaya this way, where a metered ride cost me about 1200 baht. I also took the bus to Pattaya once, but didn't really save much money because I had to take a taxi from the bus station to the hotel, and there was no taximeter.

Now, I prefer the Airport Rail Link, which gives me the feeling of really having arrived. I like sitting among the Thais and feeling like I have arrived in the middle of everyday life.

The Rail Link whizzed towards the city. I looked out of the window of the train and saw the skyline of Bangkok slowly coming into view, which made me feel almost euphoric.

Arriving in Phaya Thai, it was a bit of a strain to get to the BTS Skytrain, where I was exposed to Thailand's heat for the first time.

I took it slow, paced myself comfortably and tried to avoid any exertion. On the way, I passed a few exchange offices, which also had very good rates.

I no longer had to worry about getting a ticket for the BTS because I had a Rabbit Card.

I had bought the Rabbit Card on the recommendation of a friend. I bought the card at the counter and loaded it with credit. This card was like a permanent ticket that I just had to top up from time to time.

So, I walked proudly past the queues of tourists at the ticket counters. A few minutes later I was sitting on the BTS Skytrain.

BTS Skytrain station

2

I got off at Nana Station and walked to the Pha-chara Suites Hotel, which runs parallel to Sukhumvit on Soi 6. Barely two hours after the plane landed, I entered the hotel room.

I had booked the room at Phachara Suites Hotel a few days before via Agoda. They had really good offers and even the rooms with balconies were reasonably cheap, so I booked the first nights there.

Street scene

After checking in, I just rolled my suitcase into the room and went for a walk on Sukhumvit Road. I'd never been on a street that was so hot, noisy, dusty and hectic. But in a crazy way I felt like a million bucks, I even felt at home. I walked past bars, restaurants, tailor shops and massage parlours. The impressions can be overwhelming and I had to be careful not to get hit on the bonnet by a turning car.

At 5 pm I went into a Seven Eleven shop where I had stocked up on beer, water and cigarettes. To be on the safe side, I bought some more beer, as alcohol was only available in the shops from 5 p.m. to midnight.

Back in the room, I sat on the balcony and checked my dating apps. On Badoo and Tinder, I diligently sent out likes, and it didn't take long for me to get responses.

On WeChat, I checked if there were any nice girls in the area, but apart from a few massage ladies and ladyboys, there was nothing.

I smoked a cigarette and thought about my first evening in Bangkok.

As far as nightlife in Bangkok is concerned, there are three hotspots: Patong, Nana and Soi Cowboy. Patong is located southwest of Lumpini Park in the Bang Rag district. There is a night market, restaurants and some nightlife. But I never warmed to the area. It always seemed like a showcase for package tourists.

That's why Sukhumvit Road is my first address in Bangkok, where I can reach both Nana and Soi Cowboy on foot. For me, the area is still authentic, despite all the changes in recent years.

After getting ready to go out, I went to Sukhumvit Road. There I walked to the Artbox Night Market, which was just before Soi 10.

The market was set up like a Thai night market, but in this case more for tourists. Not a real highlight, but nice to walk around a bit. I walked past the stalls selling snacks and drinks, bought a juice and watched the live band playing there.

Then I went to Soi 8 for dinner, which was a good place for me to go in the early evening. There were a few nice restaurants, massage shops and Lolitas, a popular blowjob bar.

For the first evening, I chose the Via Vai restaurant, an Italian place where I always liked to go for dinner when I was in Bangkok. You can get very good Thai food there, but you can also get a pizza if you feel like it. For me, the main reason for going there was that the food was good.

Especially at the beginning of a holiday, I need some time to get used to everything. Who wants to sit on a bus or plane with diarrhoea when travelling on. I wasn't afraid of spoiling my stomach, which has never happened to me in street kitchens, small Thai restaurants or in the countryside. My stomach only reacts sensitively when I put it through too much at once. When I got diarrhoea, it wasn't because of the food, but because of my behaviour. If I eat spicy food, drink alcohol without end, eat a skewer on the street in between and then alcohol again ... then my stomach is overtaxed. On my first trips to Asia I thought I couldn't stomach the food, until I realised it wasn't the food, it was my eating and drinking behaviour.

After dinner, I continued towards Soi 4, where my destination was the Nana Entertainment Plaza.

When I arrived, I sat down in the beer garden to get a first impression. While enjoying my beer, I took in the surroundings. Around me, a three-storey building complex, where the go-go bars were lined up. It was garish, colourful and hot; half-naked girls and lady-boys everywhere, with people being drawn into the go-go bars. Nana is rightly considered one of the most popular male playgrounds.

After acclimatising, I walked around the complex, peeking here and there into the bars where the girls were dancing on the poles.

Suddenly, a cute mouse grabbed my hand and I let her take me to one of the bars. As I was pulled into the shop holding her hand, I admired her skinny body, covered only by white panties and a skimpy bikini top.

Nana Entertainment Plaza

The bar had a long counter on one side and a long dance floor in the middle where the girls danced on the poles. On the other side were comfortable seats, each with a table in front. The cutie led me to the seats and when I was seated, she immediately made body contact, snuggled up to me and introduced herself as Ao. The Mamasan came with a big grin and I ordered drinks for me and Ao.

When the drinks came, we toasted and afterwards her hand landed between my legs. Not wanting to be a killjoy, I joined in and felt her small breasts. Then I had her tongue in my mouth. A Ladydrink later, her hand slipped into my trousers and my fingers went under her panties. Our wild actions were interrupted at some point by the Mamasan, who wanted to introduce herself and have a drink.

I've made it a habit to buy the Mamasan a drink every now and then, because it can be damn advantageous if they like you. they are the authority par excellence for the girls. they are mummy, protector and teacher, all in one. But you have to be careful that they don't overdo it, otherwise it can get expensive. My experiences so far have been positive, with a few exceptions.

After we toasted together and had a chat, the Mamasan left. Now I turned my attention back to sweet Ao, who confessed to me that she was in love with me and that she had been waiting for someone like me for a long time. My heart soared and I wanted to hear them all, those little lies that were part of that moment, like the tongue in the throat and the grip in the trousers. That was also the time when she offered me short time for 2000 baht, which I gratefully declined. She looked up at me with sad eyes, which immediately made me feel guilty. But with another Ladydrink, I quickly made her smile again.

I realised I couldn't resist those hot bodies and her sweet ways for long, so I decided to move on to clear my head again.

Ao walked me out where we still exchanged our line ID and made me promise her that we would meet again.

I left Nana Plaza and walked up Soi 4, past the girls and ladyboys standing on the pavement offering their services. I went to Fitzgeralds, opposite Hillary 2, and sat at the long counter outside, where I could watch the hustle and bustle of the street.

I drank a beer, let the experience sink in and it calmed me down a bit between my legs. I looked straight at Hillary 2, where loud live music was playing, its bass blending with the sounds of tuk-tuks and motorbike taxis. Some pretty girls were sitting outside with their drinks and smoking.

While I was looking at Hillary and the hustle and bustle on the street, I thought about what I should do now. There was no way I could go to the hotel now. I wouldn't be able to sleep a wink in this state. So I went over to the Hillary, bought a beer at the entrance and sat down at the bar. The place was really crowded, the party people packed in, with a few drunks in between who could hardly stand up. While I was watching the band, a lady approached me and started talking to me. Her name was Nok, she quickly became trusting and openly approached me. Her friends were standing at a round table and I was persuaded to join them. Soon the girls started to show me their faces and then - what a coincidence - their drinks were empty. Nok asked me to buy a round of beers and shots.

As I already knew the Hillary 2, my alarm bells were already ringing before I joined the ladies. I made a clear announcement straight away. Buy a beer for Nok ok, nothing else and nothing for the girlfriends either. She looked at me sadly and started a discussion with me, so I said goodbye in a friendly way and sat down outside to smoke a cigarette.

In Hillary 2 I have become cautious about the lady cliques. The girls have a kind of member card with which they pay and get commission, or they take out the member card when they are invited and thus earn money on the drinks. If they get drunk with a farang and drink as much as possible, especially shots, it will be really expensive for the farang. The girls, on the other hand, not only drink for free, but also earn real money. I once spent 150 € in less than two hours at a party in this place.

In the girl bars and go-go bars, it's OK to spend money on drinks because it's part of the business model. It's transparent and they make a living out of it. But in Hillary 2 there are private girls who are just trying to get as much money out of you as possible. Of course, this doesn't apply to all the ladies there, but you should beware of groups or make clear announcements.

As I sat outside smoking a cigarette and being eyed by the lady clique, my mobile phone made itself known. Sweet Ao from the go-go Bar was calling me on Line. She wrote how much she missed me. She followed up with a selfie, looking at me like an abandoned dachshund at a motorway service station. She wanted to know where I was and what I was doing, to which I replied that I was sitting alone in the Hillary 2. In the meantime she had finished work and wanted to come and see me. I wrote back that I would be happy, and she sent me a happy emoji.

Fitzgerald with a view of Hillary 2

I had another cigarette and watched as the shop slowly emptied. In the meantime, the lady clique had picked up two young guys whom they were obviously trying hard to get; they were dancing and making out fiercely.

Then Ao came around the corner and looked at me with a bright smile. She was wearing jeans, a pullover and sneakers. I was still wondering at how she could put on a pullover in the heat when she jumped into my arms.

We sat there like a couple in love who had known each other for a long time; flirting, cuddling and saying silly things to each other. Finally, we walked to the hotel holding hands, not without getting food and drink at a Seven Eleven.

When we got to the room, we made ourselves comfortable on the balcony, ate sandwiches and had drinks; I had beer and Ao juice. We talked for a long time and she told me her story. She was from Isaan, Roi Et to be exact, had two children and was divorced. Her ex-husband was a good-for-nothing who was always out drinking. One day he left her without notice, probably because she was too old for him at 29. Now she was alone and had to see to it that her children got by.

I had often heard stories like that and they were always very sad and usually true.

It was already late at night when we went to bed after a separate shower. I was naked and she was wrapped tightly in a towel. It was hard to believe that this shy girl had been dancing lasciviously on the pole just a few hours ago.

We cuddled and kissed, whereupon bit by bit the inhibitions fell away and with them the towel. I took my time exploring her body with my tongue. As I licked her, she moved her pelvis in circular motions and clawed at the sheet. After a while, she screamed "fuck" loudly and reared back, pulling me up to her. We held each other for a moment, then I put on a rubber and slowly and gently penetrated her. I took my time, moving very slowly while she moaned in my ear. It didn't take long before I couldn't stand it any longer and came hard.

We lay like that for a while longer, our sweaty bodies clinging to each other and I savoured her scent of salty skin and desire.

It was early morning by now and I was quite tired. She snuggled tightly against me, wrapped one arm around me and was asleep in seconds, shortly and I was gone soon after.

3

When I woke up, it was only ten o'clock, but somehow I couldn't sleep any more. Ao was lying against me, still tightly embraced, as if she hadn't moved the whole time. I stroked her back and looked at her face, the most striking feature of which was her little snub nose. It didn't take long for her to wake up. The first thing she did was a spirited grab for my balls, followed by a sleepy "Good morning, darling". Of course, she immediately noticed what her delicate fingers were doing to me and once again made me happy with her hand.

While she was getting ready in the bathroom, I put 2200 baht and a bar of chocolate in her handbag, which led to more hugs, kisses and kind words as we said goodbye.

Via Soi 4, where I had breakfast, I went to the BTS Skytrain. I went to Saphan Taksin station, which was on the river. I had to change at Siam station, which was very busy at that time.

Arrived at the river, I walked straight to the boat jetty, ignored all the ticket booths and vendors until I arrived at the ticket booth for the blue boats, where I bought a ticket for small money.

My first destination was Wat Arun, a well-known temple that I could see from afar along the river. The huge conical tower, called Prang, towered impressively high and I immediately climbed it. Then I looked around the surroundings. In an outbuilding, a monk sat on a pedestal and held ceremonies with believers. They knelt in front of him, hands flat in front of their faces, while the monk pronounced a blessing and sprinkled water on the believers.

Wat Arun

I joined the group of people waiting and watched what was happening. When it was my turn, I knelt down in front of the monk, bowed three times, held my hands together flat in front of my face and looked down humbly. He spoke a few words in Thai, sprinkled water on me and tied a white ribbon around my wrist.

26

Freshly blessed, I set off to take the boat to the other side of the river. From there I went on to Wat Pho.

At 46 metres long, the reclining Buddha was so long that I barely managed to photograph it.

At the temple, I took off my shoes, took off my cap and mingled with the crowds of tourists.

Wat Pho

I took a few pictures before walking around the grounds, which was absolutely worth seeing.

Afterwards, I walked to the Royal Palace, which is touted by many travel guides as a great highlight in Bangkok, something I could never understand. I had last been there about ten years ago and wanted to give it another chance. As you can't get in there in shorts,

I wore long trousers and a long-sleeved linen shirt. In the middle of the stream, consisting of endless crowds of tourists, I went to the ticket office, paid 500 baht entrance fee and let myself be pushed into the stream of tourists. Like last time, I was disappointed.

Royal Palace

There were so many tourists that you had no chance to take in the surroundings for a moment, even though all the buildings with their impressive decorations were absolutely worth seeing. There was no atmosphere in the temple where the famous Emerald Buddha could be admired because of the crowds. So I left after less than 30 minutes.

Afterwards, I was driven to Khao San Road. The smarter way would have been across the river. You can take the blue boat to the last station and then get there after a short walk.

But I had no objection to a longer walk. I left the tuk-tuks, which were just trying to persuade me to go shopping in the area anyway, and walked to the infamous backpacker mile.

Khao San Road used to be the central meeting point for backpackers. There were cheap hostels, restaurants and parties until late at night. Actually, this has not changed until today, apart from the fact that package tourists now also cavort there.

Nearby was a small temple that I wanted to visit first. Even though I had actually seen enough temples, I enjoyed the peace and quiet that reigned there. There was nothing pompous here, it was rather the simplicity that made me feel comfortable and made me stay there for a while.

Khao San Road

Afterwards, I strolled through the alleys in the area, past small boutiques and restaurants, until I finally stopped for a coffee break on Khao San Road.

Backpackers strolled through the street, looking curiously and shocked at a barbecue cart offering freshly prepared insects. Every now and then a tuk-tuk drove by, in a boutique a saleswoman lovingly draped some T-shirts in the display.

Chilled jazz music came from a restaurant across the street. In front of it sat a group of young people eating Thai curry and drinking beer.

Now I was getting tired and decided to go back to the hotel. As it was rush hour, I took a taxi to the nearest BTS Station and took the Skytrain the rest of the way. If the taxi had taken me directly to the hotel, it would have taken me half an hour longer because of the traffic jams.

When I was in the room, I looked at my mobile phone and found seventeen messages from Ao. She sent pictures, love notes and stickers. I replied with a few curt comments and then got ready for the evening.

I was going to the Ratchathewi district. I took the BTS to the station of the same name and went to Co-cowalk. I first walked around, looked at the restaurants, where the atmosphere was very relaxed. Finally, I decided on the Chilling House Café, where I made myself comfortable with a view of the stage.

After dinner, I stayed there for a good two hours watching the live band playing a nice mix of pop and jazz. I didn't want to move, it was so cosy.

I finally got myself together and took the BTS two stops further, to the Victory Monument. In a corner building, where there was a restaurant, there was the Skytrain Jazz Bar on the roof. Certainly not one of the big highlights in Bangkok, but I liked it very much for that very reason. A small place in vintage style, far away from any mainstream. This bar was apparently not very well known among tourists, there were almost exclusively young Thais there who looked like students. I didn't have the amazing view of the Bangkok skyline, but I was in the middle of a rustic lounge atmosphere that I didn't often find.

I had a beer and watched people talking, laughing, smoking cigarettes and drinking beer or whisky.

A beer and a cigarette later, I left because I wanted to go to the Saxophone Bar. I walked towards the Victory Monument and turned right into a side street before the roundabout. After a few metres I saw the fairy lights and the sign saying "Jack Lives Here.

I entered the bar, which is one of the hottest jazz clubs in town. I was warmly welcomed and taken to a seat at the side of the stage. It wasn't the most ideal seat, but I was close to the stage and got to see everything up close. It was packed, the audience was international; here, a large part was made up of tourists.

The band was a real hit. They played together so confidently and groovily that it gave me goosebumps. Every single musician was an absolute professional. During the solo parts, the audience literally held its breath.

I stayed there for three beers and let myself drift with the music.

Saxophone-Bar

As the BTS Skytrain only ran until midnight, I took a taxi back to Sukhumvit Road. I didn't go to the hotel, but wanted to have a nightcap somewhere and was taken to Nana Plaza. This time I didn't go in, but sat down opposite at Hooters, where you can sit at a long counter and watch the street, just like at Fitzgerald.

It is one of the most entertaining places in Bangkok's nightlife. You have a view of the entrance area of Nana Plaza, but you can also watch the easy girls and ladyboys offering their services on the street.

It is one of the most entertaining places in Bangkok's nightlife. You have a view of the entrance area of Nana Plaza, but you can also watch the easy girls and ladyboys offering their services on the street.

Diagonally opposite was Bigdogs, where I had often been and had good experiences with the girls. I often sat there, had a drink with a lady, watched the traffic and talked.

Next door was the Stumble Inn, also a nice place, but too noisy for my taste.

There was also the Hillary 4. I never saw any rip-off girl cliques there, just bar girls.

View from Hooters to Nana entrance area

Next to me sat an Englishman who introduced himself as Henry. We chatted while curiously watching the girls on the pavement.

Of course, we were also noticed and now some of the girls started flirting with us. First a slight, barely perceptible smile that seemed almost shy, then more offensive, up to a few cheeky sayings. But I wanted to go to bed alone tonight and Henry was undecided.

One of the girls finally went all out, came up to us and went straight for Henry. She stood indecent-ly close to him and said she would go with him. He seemed overwhelmed, thanked her for the offer and told her he didn't want to. She didn't let up and asked him if she was too ugly or something else was wrong with her. In doing so, she put good Henry in a quandary, who had to watch that he didn't inadvertently offend her. Losing face is a huge issue in Thailand, so small misunderstandings can often have a big impact. Henry, however, did an excellent job of getting out of it by complimenting her and explaining that it just wasn't right for him at the moment. Somewhat disappointed, she pulled away and went back to posing on the pavement.

Henry now confessed to me that he had a crush on one of the girls and pointed to a lovely creature sitting on a parked moped. This creature was in-deed a feast for the eyes, with a white dress, high heels and an elegance and grace rarely seen in Thai women. He was now really desperate because she totally ignored him, any attempt at flirtation or even a smile, came to nothing.

I shared with him my theory as to why he was so mercilessly ignored. This charming creature was a ladyboy who knew exactly that Henry didn't see it. The ladyboy himself, I'm sure, just wanted to avoid an embarrassing situation with loss of face, so he was on the lookout for men who were specifically looking for transgenders. Henry looked at me as if I had pulled a beer bottle over his head. He was totally shocked that he had just fallen for a guy. Now he wanted to know how I could tell, or by what characteristics I had spotted it. But it wasn't easy for me to explain.

There are some features like big hands and feet, larynx etc., but none of them are really reliable. I am always suspicious when a woman is super sexy or moves gracefully on high heels. It's a sad truth that most Thai women can't move sexily on high heels and their gait looks like that of a waddling duck. Lots of make-up is also a warning sign for me, as are perfectly proportioned breasts.

You can only be really sure if you take a look at the identity card. There, the sex is written as it was at birth and will never be changed, not even in the case of a complete change of sex.

I reassured him afterwards that I often didn't recognise it myself. I once met a lady in a bar with whom I had a great time. We drank, had fun and made out violently. I was so horny for her that spending the night together was out of the question. That's when she confessed to me that she was a ladyboy. It was an extremely awkward situation, but I was grateful that he told me in time. I have often heard of stories where the big surprise came in bed.

It should be enough for the night and I make my way back to the hotel to get a few more hours of sleep than I did last night.

4

After a night of sleeping like a rock, I wanted to explore the shopping malls, so I took the BTS to Siam Station. From there I went to the MBK Centre where I treated myself to a new phone cover. I also took the opportunity to get the bulletproof glass replaced.

Then I went to the 4th floor to get some cash from a yellow Krungsri Bank ATM, a bank I always prefer. If there is no Krungsri ATM available, I try Krung Thai or Bangkok Bank. With some banks you have to be very careful if they offer to settle at their own exchange rate. You should always choose "no" as withdrawing money can be expensive due to a worse exchange rate. I have never had any problems with my regular banks.

The MBK Centre used to be considered an insider tip. But as it is with insider tips, they are no longer secret as soon as they appear somewhere as an insider tip. Despite the increasing number of shops catering to tourists, the mall has somehow managed to retain its charm.

From the MBK Centre, I went over to the Siam Discovery. For a few years now, the two malls have been connected by a skywalk, which is a highlight in itself.

I stayed here for a while and took a few pictures. There was street traffic below, the BTS Skytrain snaked along the skywalk and the malls loomed in the background.

Skywalk MBK

Via Siam Discovery and Siam Center, I went to Siam Paragon. All three malls are quite expensive and not exactly made for the poor. However, Bangkok is comparatively expensive anyway. I continued on the Skywalk to the Erawan Shrine, which gained sad notoriety due to the attacks in 2015. I have often stood here on the skywalk and watched the Hindu ceremonies. It is such a peaceful atmosphere that it never entered my mind how someone could detonate a bomb in this place.

38

From there it was a stone's throw to Central World. A huge shopping centre with a department store attached to it. I got lost there countless times. Every time I thought I had it, I ended up in a new corner and got lost again. This time, however, I found my way quite well. I browsed in a bookshop, looked for CDs and looked for bargains on sportswear.

Central World

Right next to Central World is a temple called Wat Pathum Wanaram, which I also wanted to visit. It's an oasis of calm in the midst of the city's hustle and bustle. Buddhist ceremonies are held there every day at 6pm and everyone is welcome. I attended one once, which involved a lot of sitting and lasted over two hours. The temple also has a small garden where you can relax or try walking meditation.

I took the Skywalk past Central World to the Platinum Mall. Everything was a bit simpler, cheaper and more authentic here. This was where the locals shopped. The night market in front of the mall is very popular with Thais as well as tourists. But it was too busy for me, so I went straight to the Palladium Mall, on the other side of the intersection.

The Palladium Mall was less crowded and much more relaxed. But the real reason I went to this mall was for the massages. It's not cheaper than anywhere else, but the massages were always top notch.

As soon as I arrived at the mall, I was picked up by a massage fairy and led to a matress. A wonderful massage followed, the likes of which I have only experienced in a few places in Bangkok. The massages there are mostly serious, which means the ladies are usually not pushy. Only once was I offered a hand job. But that was the exception, the lady was obviously interested in me.

After the massage I visited the relatively new shopping centre "The Market". It was on the way back to Central World, accessible via the skywalk on the left. This mall is one of my favourites, as inconspicuous as it is. There was not much going on, everything was very relaxed, ideal for strolling. I bought a shirt in a boutique that you don't see on every corner.

After that I had a coffee and got a bit lazy. So I went back to the hotel to rest.

I had lots of messages from Ao, who wanted to see me again. We chatted a bit without me promising her anything.

In the evening I went to Asoke, Terminal 21; a shopping mall that is very popular with the Thais. Each floor is designed to resemble a city, with its landmarks. On one floor you are in Istanbul, on another in San Francisco.

Terminal 21

But this time I wasn't here for sightseeing and shopping. The destination was the food court, an area with lots of kitchens where you had an inexhaustible choice of food. I went to the cashier, got a 300 baht card and then ordered some delicious stuff that looked good but I had no idea what it was. After eating I went to the famous Terminal 21 toilet. They have Japanese toilets in the mall that have an electric ass shower and are heated. After stuffing myself and emptying myself it was almost 10 pm, time for the nightlife.

As I was already in the area, I decided to pay a visit to Soi Cowboy. It wasn't far to walk and as I stood at the start of this little fun mile, I soaked up the wicked atmosphere. First I sat down in the outdoor area of Country Road, where I had a good view of the action. Colourful bright lights, lots of girls in mini-skirts and astonished tourists.

I decided to stop off at a go-go bar to get in the mood. I went to Tilac, whose interior I liked; the lighting was pleasant, the ambience modern. I soon had a bunny sitting next to me. I bought her a drink and we chatted. She wasn't nearly as devoted as Ao, in fact nothing came from her at all. She was pretty, no doubt. She had dyed blonde hair, an extremely skinny figure and, for a Thai, quite large breasts. Out of curiosity I asked her how much it would cost if she came with me for longtime. She said 6000 baht for the whole night. I almost spat out my beer in shock, it was over 150 €. But I shouldn't have been surprised, after all Soi Cowboy is much more expensive than Nana. However, it was not a given that Ao would be happy with 2000 plus tip. Go-go girls are more expensive than bar girls or freelancers. I didn't even ask about barfine. In go-go bars it is easily 1000 baht and more, which would have been no different here.

It didn't really work out between us. Sometimes you don't dislike each other, but somehow the chemistry isn't right. It doesn't make sense to rush into anything, especially at such prices.

Then I walked down Soi Cowboy and thought about going to Crazy House. This is the most popular go-go bar in Bangkok, or at least it's the one that people rave about the most. I didn't think the bar was bad, but the girls weren't cheap either, as I'd experienced a year before.

Soi Cowboy

Now it was time to change the territory and I walked along Sukhumvit Road again. Every now and then I was approached by a freelancer, but none of them caught my eye. In the dark it wasn't easy to see what they looked like or if there was a ladyboy hiding behind them.

Then I passed the Ruamchitt Hotel, where the Thermae Café was in the basement. From a distance I could see all the pretty girls lined up outside. Somehow the sight gave me an appetite and I went down the stairs. After getting a beer, I stood at the front for a moment and took in the scene. Lots of pretty young girls were standing side by side, offering themselves.

There are no professionals working at Thermae Café. The girls who offer their services are there privately and just want to supplement their pocket money. They usually have normal jobs or are studying. When they are broke or need a new mobile phone, they go to Thermae and look for someone to go with them for money. You can also tell that the girls there are private by the fact that they are so damn selective. Europeans hardly stand a chance against the Asian tourists.

There are many theories as to why the girls prefer Asians. Personally, I think Asians are more generous. Furthermore, the girls feel more comfortable if they are already involved with a foreign man.

Like the other lecherous sacks, I joined the crowd and walked in a circle to get a closer look at the girls. Most of them ignored me or even looked away demonstratively to show that they were not interested in me. But some of the girls looked right at me and smiled, which was a pretty cool feeling. I felt like I had been chosen when such a beautiful girl smiled at me.

My mind started to shut down again and I had to get out to clear my head. I walked down Sukhumvit to the sports bar "The Game", where I first went to the toilet and had a freshly tapped beer.

While watching a football match on the screen, I thought about going back to Thermae. Some of the girls were pretty as hell, and there was hardly a better choice outside the go-go bars.

Thermae Café

So I traipsed back down the stairs, had a beer and went for the next round. It was late and fortunately the place was not so full. There were even a few seats free. I shuffled through the shop, looking at the girls, most of whom turned their heads away again. The one or two MILFs who had squeezed in smiled at me, and I was the one who looked away. All in all, there was too much choice and I couldn't decide.

Then I stood at a table in the middle of the shop and looked around. As I looked around, I noticed two eyes focused on me. These eyes belonged to a very sweet girl in a short white dress with a floral pattern. She had a top figure, long black hair and discreet make-up. Her gaze rested on me without turning away for a second. All the men were ignored, which amazed me, almost creepy in this shop. An Asian man approached her, but she just shook her head without looking at him.

I smiled and pointed to the seat next to me and she came over and sat down. Her name was Phan, she was 34 years old and worked in a hairdressing salon. Her age surprised me, I would have guessed she was in her mid-20s. We hit it off, she was ambitious, athletic and knew what she wanted. She wasn't in a hurry, telling me a lot about herself as she thoughtfully cuddled my forearm.

I asked Phan if she wanted to come with me and she nodded. She wanted 3000 baht, which was too much for me, despite my sympathy. But we quickly agreed on 2000 baht and went to the hotel holding hands.

She accompanied me into the shower and soaped me tenderly, which made me quite hot. I couldn't keep my fingers still, feeling her breasts and ass. Then we kissed, her hands moving down to my balls.

We didn't dry ourselves properly, so we got half wet on the bed and made out like crazy. She started to suck me tenderly. First she ran her tongue over my glans, then she wrapped her lips around it and took it deep into her mouth. Phan now put a rubber on me, sat on top of me and began to move her pelvis slowly as she leaned forward and pressed her lips greedily onto mine. She moved faster and moaned in rhythm with her movements, I grabbed her hips and continued to press her firmly against me. Then we turned over and I lay on top of her, speeding up and finally coming noisily to the end.

We lay awake for a long time, half naked on top of each other, and talked. She peppered me with questions about her wife, children and job, but also told me a lot about herself and her plans for the future. I stroked her taut upper body and felt a little sad that such a woman lived 10,000 kilometres away from me. No sooner had I finished thinking than I fell asleep.

5

After a day of temples and shopping, I wanted to go green this time. I went to the Ban Kachao peninsula, also known as the green lung of Bangkok. It started with a really stupid mistake. I got into a taxi thinking I was going straight to the peninsula. It looked easy on the map, but the journey took forever because we had to make a huge loop. When we arrived at Ban Kachao, I was surprised at the size of the peninsula. I had actually thought about exploring it all on foot, but I quickly changed my mind.

I was taken to the floating market, which I had heard a lot about. When the driver dropped me off, I was standing in the middle of nowhere. The taxi driver pointed out a path for me to follow. With no other choice, I took him at his word. There were no taxis or tuk-tuks to be seen, just like in a village in the countryside. I wondered how I was going to get out of here and walked along the path the driver had pointed out. But after a short while I arrived at my destination with a slightly uneasy feeling.

When I entered the market, it had been worth the effort. It was very authentic and natural. It gave me a real Isaan feeling. It was hard to believe that so close to this noisy and smoky city, everything could be so green and quiet. The people here were also completely different from those a few kilometres further north. Hardly anyone spoke English, but everyone was friendly. I walked around the market twice, looking curiously at the food on offer and trying a few things myself. I like to eat things I don't know what they are. In Thailand, everything has been delicious so far - except the durian fruit, which smells like a fart after a plate of beans.

Now I wanted to go to the nature park, which had to be somewhere in the area. There was just one problem ... how should I get away from here? I looked around the market and thought. Then I noticed where most of the people were coming from and in which direction most of them were going. I followed the people and soon found myself in a car park. A granite block fell from my heart when I saw a group of motorbike taxi drivers. Luckily, they immediately understood what I wanted, and within minutes I was at the entrance to the nature park.

Right at the entrance I borrowed a bicycle and set off. At this place I was in pure nature, where I felt like I was in a jungle. I could hardly believe that there was such a jungle in the middle of this metropolis.

I walked through winding paths, over a pier and finally climbed a lookout tower. From the top,

however, I could see nothing but the jungle that surrounded me.

I met many young Thais on a day trip. The nature
park is a popular diversion for stressed city people.

Ban Kachao nature park

When I got back to the entrance, I satisfiedly returned the bike and looked around for motorbike
taxis. Again, I had been worried for nothing as there
were a few of them near the entrance. This time I decided on a woman, walked up to her and explained
that I needed to get to the centre but had no idea how
to get there. She just said "no problem", so I got in and
was soon at my next destination. She had dropped me
off at a jetty from where I was taken across the river
on a klong boat for 10 baht. On the other side, tuk-
tuks were waiting to take me to Lumpini Park.

Lumpini Park is impressively large for its central location. It's the ideal place to get away from it all if you want to escape the hustle and bustle. It's a great place to relax or exercise. The conditions are ideal for joggers and cyclists.

When the sun goes down, crowds of runners gather here to do their laps at a leisurely pace. The park is also easily accessible by BTS, which goes to the river.

While I was walking through the park, I spotted a monitor lizard. The creature was at least a metre long and crawling comfortably across the grass. I approached it, but kept a respectful distance and watched the creature. It paid no attention to me, crawled leisurely to the lake and slid into the water.

Lumpini Park

To the north-east of the park I went out onto the Green Mile.

The Green Mile is a cycle and footpath that leads directly to Benjakitti Park. Like a bridge, the path connects the two parks.

Although it is advertised as an insider tip in many travel guides, I never noticed many tourists there. I really like this walk because it shows the contrasts of Bangkok. You walk past simple houses and behind them the towering skyscrapers.

View from the Green Mile

I looked down and saw people going about their day. A woman had just started a washing machine. In one house there was a makeshift shop where you could buy the things you needed every day. An old man lay sleeping on what looked like a veranda. The people here were certainly anything but rich. This made the view of the skyscrapers where the rich lived all the more disconcerting.

When I reached Benjakitti Park, the sun was slowly setting. I liked this park even more than Lumpini Park because the view of Bangkok's skyline was breathtaking. I waited until the sun had set and then went for a walk to admire this incredibly impressive skyline.

Sweaty and bitten by mosquitoes, I made my way back to the hotel.

Benjakitti Park

Freshly showered, I strolled up Sukhumvit Road to Soi 14. I turned into the Soi and after a few steps my destination appeared on the right. The Suda Restaurant, a Thai restaurant where I was a regular.

I ordered a curry and had a water with it. The food was exceptionally good and I enjoyed eating traditional food again. This restaurant had the typical character of street food. The first time I went there I was worried that I wouldn't be able to stomach it, but my worries were unfounded. The only downer about this restaurant is its popularity. It is usually full and they try to get guests through quickly. Sitting comfortably for two hours is not appreciated.

Well satiated, but without feeling full, I walked to Sukhumvit on the side of the odd soi. I started on Soi 7, where there were a few street bars right at the beginning. Makeshift tables and a few plastic stools were about it. As rudimentary as these street bars are, I always stop at one from time to time. The simplicity of the asphalt, the rubbish and the rats make me feel grounded. I've often met a nice girl here and picked her up.

But today I went and checked out the new bar district. It was so new that not every bar was open. This area was built to replace the demolished Queens Park in Soi 22.

I sneaked around the bars where the girls were friendly but unobtrusive, very sympathetic. I spontaneously stopped at a bar where I was greeted by an extremely friendly lady.

She was about 30 years old, pretty, with a bit of flab on her hips. As the only customer, I got her full attention and was immediately well looked after.

I ordered a beer and a Ladydrink for her, and we chatted. She told me how bad it was in the bar, hardly any customers, never anything going on. It wasn't hard for me to believe. Apart from three or four bars, there was nothing going on here at all. On the other hand, I also had the feeling that the old bar district was a ghost town. The atmosphere wasn't bad at all, nice modern design, unobtrusive lighting and a lovely lady. Nevertheless, I didn't want to spend the whole evening here, so I left.

Outside I went to the beer garden where the hottest milfs in Bangkok are picked up.

The beer garden is a kind of large pub. The atmosphere is more like a brewery, except that they don't brew beer. Middle-aged women sit there from early afternoon until late at night. These ladies hang around looking for tourists to accompany them for pocket money. Opinions vary on the quality of the women. So far I have always had good experiences with the place. I even picked up a really pretty 24-year-old there once.

I went for a spin around the shop and felt like a rock star. The ladies adored me and tried to be on their best behaviour. I sat down at a counter and ordered a beer. I thought the girls would jump on me at any moment. It was obvious that there was a lot of wooing going on. The competition was obvious.

One lady who had almost sucked me in at the entrance tapped me on the shoulder. Before I could react, she was sitting next to me and talking without taking a breath. She was trying to convince me of her merits. She stuck out her breasts, felt me up and told me what a handsome guy I was. Somehow, though, she wasn't my case and I kindly told her it wasn't going to work. She accepted without complaint and disappeared as quickly as she had appeared to take her place at the entrance for the next visitor.

Now my eyes caught sight of an extremely sympathetic appearance, just a few feet from me. She was wearing a white shirt, jeans and flat shoes. She used make-up sparingly, but still looked good. I liked her unassuming, almost shy manner. I smiled at her, asked how she was, and she replied in a friendly manner, asking a few standard questions like "are you on holiday?" or "are you travelling alone?". When we were finished with the opening sentences, I asked her to sit with me. As she stood up, I noticed that the body was also nice to look at.

We had a drink together and had an excellent conversation. Her English was not very good, but as I knew a bit of Thai myself, we got by with a mixture of English and Thai.

Her name was Chan, she was 38 years old and from Bangkok. She worked in a cookshop, where she earned only a little money.

She also came here to earn some pocket money. She told me that she was very rarely in the beer garden, and I believed her. In any case, I had never seen her before. Tentative touches on the arm or leg accompanied the conversation, like a normal flirt.

Now I offered her to go somewhere else to have another drink. She agreed and I asked one of the staff for the bill. As I only had large notes left, I put a 1000 Baht note on the counter and photographed it so that the barman it. When he took the note, I said again clearly that it was 1000 baht. Normally I never do this, but in the beer garden I had already had trouble twice with the scam that I gave 1000, the barman was gone for 10 minutes and then gave it to me for 500.

We walked hand in hand down Sukhumvit towards Asoke. We passed Soi 7/1, which is "the" street for blowjob bars and brothels. Then we turned into Soi 11, where on the left was Zanzibar. A beer garden where you can have a drink in a relaxed atmosphere with chilly live music.

We had a beer, watched the band and chatted. She told us about herself and her family, and we became more and more familiar with each other's looks and touches.

The mood became more relaxed and at one point she asked me if I knew the Havana Club on Soi 11. I had heard of it but had never been there. We finished our beer and made our way up the Soi.

The club was unremarkable from the outside, I had never noticed it before. There was a telephone in front of the door, Chan entered a number, the door opened and I thought I had landed in Havana. Salsa music filled my ears. It was dark and pretty rustic. The club was modelled on a Cuban bar. I could hardly believe I was still in Asia.

Havanna social

We sat down at the bar, ordered beers and watched the people. Many of the visitors were wearing Caribbean hats, some couples had dressed up really well. Women in elegant dresses that you would normally only expect to see at fancy cocktail parties. The men dressed smartly, with a proud and confident air. What they were doing wasn't just for show, they could really dance. Their movements were fluid and rhythmic, the mood was exuberant.

We watched the spectacle for a while until we decided to go back to the hotel and end the evening with a little togetherness.

When we got to the hotel room, we showered separately. When I came out of the bathroom, I put on some South American lounge music on my tablet and smoked a cigarette on the balcony while she showered.

When she came out, I was delighted by the sight of her. Her body was very nice to look at, even without clothes. Small but firm breasts, slim and freshly shaved.

We lay down on the bed and the restrained, shy lady became a real wildcat. We made out tentatively at first, then more and more wildly, the kisses becoming more and more demanding and wet. She slid down to suck me off. She enjoyed it very much, taking it deep into her mouth and making smacking noises. Then she stroked her tongue over my balls, licking them greedily before taking my cock deep into her mouth again. Her tongue moved down and massaged my underside. Then she opened my ass cheeks and touched my anus with the tip of her tongue. She really seemed to enjoy it. She didn't stop, skillfully tonguing my anus, then licking my balls and going down again with her tongue. She massaged my wet cock and looked into my eyes from time to time.

Finally I couldn't stand it any longer and reached for the rubber on the bedside table. She bent over in front of me in doggy style and I pushed my cock into her cunt from behind. She moaned and held it tight, then I picked up the pace and thrust harder, whereupon she threw back her head and let out cries of pleasure.

We switched again and I took her in the missy. Again, I pushed slowly at first, then more and more wildly. She moaned loudly, pinching my nipples until I finally came violently.

We sat on the balcony, had a beer together and talked. Talking with her was very pleasant. She had a lot of life experience, which made her quite detached and relaxed about life. She was well-informed about politics and world affairs and also had a clear and reasonable opinion, which I liked.

As we lay in bed, I put on the South American music and fell asleep to the images of Havana Club.

6

We woke up at almost the same time in the morning. I looked at Chan, who was also awake, her eyes rested on me. A satisfied smile was on her lips. Her hand wandered down my body to between my legs, where something was about to stir again. Without saying anything, she slid down my body to suck me again. She followed the same procedure as the night before, licking my anus extensively. I didn't really feel like it this morning, but she had made me horny again with her tongue. I grabbed the next rubber and finished with a quickie in the missy.

After saying goodbye to Chan with a reasonable amount of pocket money, 2000 baht as usual, I checked my mobile phone messages and noticed that there were 13 messages from Ao. I replied again curtly, but this time she didn't let up and a video call came through Line. She was smiling into the camera, telling me how much she missed me and how much she wanted to see me again. I told her that it was my last day in Bangkok and that I would be leaving the next day, whereupon she looked at me with big sad eyes.

When she asked what else I had planned for the day, I told her that sightseeing was on the agenda. She just said "ok, I'll go with you" and half an hour later, she was standing in front of the hotel.

Ao asked me if I wanted to see anything in particular, but I just said I wanted to see some temples. She decided to be my guide for the day, took my hand and we walked to the BTS Station. When I asked her how long she had, she just said as long as I wanted. When I asked her when she had to go to the go-go bar, she replied that she had stopped working. I was surprised and curious but got nothing out of her. She just said she had decided to go home and changed the subject. As a matter of course, she held my hand and we chatted as familiarly as if we had always been a couple.

We drove out of town to Punnawithi station, went to a family market and bought gifts for the monks. Then we went to Wat Dhammamongkol, a tower temple little known to tourists. She led me straight to a monk who was holding sessions for the faithful. We knelt before him, bowed three times and Ao gave him the gifts. Then they talked for a while, of which I understood almost nothing. Then came the ceremony where he blessed us and sprinkled water on us.
Finally he tied a red ribbon around our wrists.

Wat Dhammamongkol

Then we looked around and went into the main temple. There were only Thais praying or meditating. We took mats and sat down a bit apart. Ao had her eyes closed and seemed to be praying, her lips moving silently.

I would like to go up the tower to take some pictures from the top, but the lift was broken. When I tried to go up the stairs, she pulled me away and said it was not a good time. I gave in, knowing that Thai girls are not very good on their feet. If I had pushed her up the stairs, the tour would have been over.

Outside, Ao organised a tuk-tuk and we continued to the next temple. We drove towards Ekkamai and then turned off to Wat Pase, a temple near the canal.

Wat Pase

The temple was nothing special from the outside, there were hardly any people around, but there was a lot to learn here.

Ao explained all sorts of things to me about Buddhist rituals. We poured oil into a bowl and lit a wick in the middle of the bowl. Then we put money into a machine which spat out a blessing to bring us luck and prosperity. Finally, we crawled through a tunnel inside the building. The squatting position was to teach us humility. She explained everything to me with great enthusiasm and I took it all in gratefully.

Afterwards we went to the canal and waited at the pier for the next boat. We didn't have to wait long and walked a few stops to the Jim Thompson House.

Canal

The Jim Thompson House is a museum I've never been to, despite its high profile. We took a guided tour, listened to the lady's explanations and waited until it was over. The house was interesting, but I was more interested in Thai culture, which I didn't really find here. Ao had probably taken me there because she thought I would be interested. She seemed bored herself.

Jim Thompson House

By mutual agreement we went back to the canal to continue our journey by boat.

Our next destination was the Golden Mount Temple. It was a temple on top of a small mountain with a magnificent view over Bangkok.

When we arrived, Ao said I should go up alone and she would wait for me at the bottom. I didn't want to do that this time, so I took the mouse by the hand and dragged her behind me like a wet sack. By the time we were halfway up, her nagging had subsided and at the first platform she pulled out her mobile phone and enthusiastically took selfies. At the top we followed another ritual, which my mouse explained to me in detail. I took a place setting, which consisted of a folded cloth on a bowl, and walked around the chedi, the conical top of the temple, three times. Then I placed the set at the base of the chedi. Ao watched me proudly and took lots of pictures of me. Then it was her turn and I took some pictures of her too.

As I looked at her, I realised how good she made me feel. She looked after me with such devotion that it was almost touching. I was convinced that she was a very good mother. I looked at her pretty face, her little snub nose, her petite body and noticed that somehow my stomach started to tingle. This was not good ... not good at all.

We settled down against the outside wall and sat close together on the floor. We looked at the pictures and talked, while seat mats were laid out and the first people sat down for evening prayers. The sun was approaching the horizon and the monks came to perform the ceremony.

We discussed what we wanted to do for the evening and I suggested that we could go out for a fancy dinner and then I wanted to go to a sky bar.

After some back and forth, I suggested Lebua Tower. I've always wanted to go there, but either I didn't have the opportunity or I didn't have the right company. Ao warned me that it would be expensive, but I didn't care. I felt good, everything fit, I hadn't spent much money yet either... so I wanted to have a good time.

Golden Mount (Wat Saket)

We took the tuk-tuk to her flat, which she shared with a friend. You couldn't really call it a very simple flat, it was just a living room where they slept on mattresses. There was a small balcony off the front. They didn't have air conditioning, but there were two fans in the corners to fight the tropical heat.

It took Ao ages to get ready. She had never been to Lebua Tower before and it was a special highlight for her too. When she finally came out of the bathroom, I was blown away. She was wearing a red silk dress. The dress came up to just above her knees and was blowing slightly to the side in the breeze from the fans. The neckline gave a glimpse of the base of her breasts without showing too much. She was wearing high-heeled black pumps. The sight made me horny, but what I most wanted to do would have been a bad idea now.

On the drive to the hotel, she thanked me for my compliments and chatted with the taxi driver, who was curious to know what we were doing that evening.

While I had a shower and gathered the best clothes I could find in my suitcase, Ao booked a table at Sirocco restaurant. We had some time and sat on the balcony, chatting, holding hands and looking at pictures of the restaurant and bar we were going to that night.

As soon as the taxi pulled up at Lebua Tower, we were greeted like celebrities. The staff met us directly at the taxi and escorted us inside to the lift. When we entered the restaurant, we were immediately greeted and escorted to our table. They treated us like a princess. I was sure they knew what kind of establishment I'd picked them up at, but they didn't let on.

Classical music was performed by a string quartet. They played many well-known pieces by Mozart, Bach, Mendelsohn and some other celebrities. Ao couldn't relate to the music, but she loved the stylish ambience and the fantastic view of the Bangkok skyline.

We were given the menus and the prices shot into my eyes like arrows. Somehow I didn't care at that moment, I had 20,000 baht and two credit cards in case of need. We ordered a four-course meal, a glass of white wine and a bottle of water.

Before and between courses we were treated to small culinary delights from the kitchen, so that in the end there were actually seven courses. But the treats were more like snacks. Freshly baked bread was served in between, which was delicious. Each course was announced with great fanfare and they explained what it was. As I have no idea about food and my English vocabulary is correspondingly poor, I only understood half of it. It was mostly European and Australian specialities. Every single course was a delight, Ao was ecstatic and photographed every detail with her mobile phone.

Although the portions were not particularly generous, I was still full. This was partly because they gave us bread without end and partly because the dessert was a calorie bomb. It was too much for my mouse and she fed me her dessert.

When we finished eating, Ao thanked me so heartily. She was so excited that tears welled up in her eyes, and at that moment I knew it was the right decision, even at that crazy price.

When she went to the toilet, I had the bill brought to me. I was relieved to find that my cash was easily enough. But I paid by credit card to have enough cash for the onward journey. My destination for the next day was Ayutthaya and I wasn't sure there would be an ATM on every corner.

We made a detour to the famous Skybar to have another of their sinfully expensive cocktails.

Lebua Tower

As we stepped out I held my breath. A wide staircase led down to the bar, which was set off by subtle ambient lighting. Behind it was the skyline of Bangkok, with the Chao Phraya River snaking through. A friendly staff member took some photos of us with the skyline in the background. Ao couldn't get enough pictures and wanted to be photographed in every pose imaginable.

Then we ordered cocktails at the bar. Ao was blissful and thanked me endlessly for the evening. She cuddled up to me and kept nudging me with her nose.

Skybar on Lebua Tower

While we were taking the taxi back to the hotel, I was thinking how crazy it was to have spent so much money. The evening cost me over 400 €, but it was worth it. It was a unique experience that I knew I would remember for a long time.

When we reached the hotel room, I took off my shoes, put my things on the table and looked at Ao, who was looking at me seriously. She fixed me, no, fixed me with her eyes, came over and kissed me. We lay down on the bed and I stroked her dress, sliding my hand down her cleavage. I felt her breasts, the nipples of which were very hard. She kissed me wetly, sliding her tongue greedily into my mouth, while my hand slid down her dress, stroking the inside of her thigh, then up to her panties. She reached right between my legs, unzipped my trousers and bravely reached inside. We were so hot for each other at that moment that I was afraid I was going to come.

Then we undressed, leaving her panties on. I explored her body with my hand while she stroked my cock. Then I kissed her breasts and played with her hard nipples with my tongue. When I moved my lips down over her belly, she laid her head back and moaned in pleasure. I kissed her pussy through her panties, which I then pulled off. Freshly shaved, she opened her legs and let me in. I kissed her labia and then licked them gently with the tip of my tongue. I slid my fingertip between her lips and felt how wet she was. Now I began to lick her as she moaned lustfully and looked down at me again and again. She held her pussy apart with her fingers as I licked her and gently inserted a finger inside her. After a few minutes she reared up and pressed her pussy firmly against my face. I gave in a little and she pushed my head against her pussy. She moaned loudly, it almost sounded like she was having a crying fit.

Her breathing slowed and her body relaxed. I slid between her legs, hugged her and we kissed.

I took a rubber and as I put it on she smiled and said I was a good man. I thanked her with a kiss and slowly penetrated her. She wrapped her legs around me and I began to move inside her. Very gently and deeply I moved inside her, then I became faster, she became more demanding and started moaning loudly again. After a while she realised I was ready and cheered me on with "fuck me". It didn't take long and I had a huge orgasm.

We stayed in this position for a while, our bodies wet with sweat, my heart still racing.

Ao asked me if I wanted something to drink, but I wasn't thirsty. She said she wanted to treat me, and I finally agreed to a beer. She went to the fridge, took out a beer, filled it ceremoniously into a glass and handed it to me submissively. Then she took a water for herself and lay down with me.

For a while we lay there, wordless, caressing each other, each in our own thoughts. Then I took the iPad and asked her to search for Isaan music on YouTube. She was pleased that I liked Isaan music, and soon the happy rhythmic sounds of a traditional Thai song came on. She lay in my arms, kissed me in between and then cuddled up to me again.

At some point she told me in Thai that she loved me. I said in Thai that I loved her and kissed her. She opened her mouth and slipped her tongue between my lips, her hand slipping back between my legs. As life awoke in me again, she slid down me, brushing her body over my cock, which felt like it was about to burst. Then she took it in her hand and guided it into her mouth. I watched as her tongue and lips played with me with pleasure. Then she took a rubber, put it on me and sat on me. She inserted my cock and pushed her pelvis down in rhythmic movements. I felt her hug me, caress her breasts and hold on to them. She leaned forward, pressed her lips to my mouth and kissed me more and more wildly. She rode me faster, thrusting her pelvis hard against mine. I gripped her hips with both hands and supported her movements by pushing her down hard against me. It took longer this time, but finally I came again. I felt more satisfied than I had in a long time.

Afterwards, as she lay in my arms, she wanted to know how long I had left for my holiday and when I would be back in Bangkok. I told her it wouldn't be long and that we would see each other soon. She said she would wait for me no matter how long it took.

7

When I woke up, Ao was lying half on top of me. Her head rested peacefully on my chest. She woke up shortly after me and looked at me with her sleepy eyes. Then she pressed her pelvis against my side and put her hand on my hip, and I immediately got hard again. So in the morning we continued what we had finished at night, and some time later we lay sweating against each other.

Then we took turns to shower. While Ao was in the bathroom, I put the pocket money and a bar of chocolate in her handbag and checked hotels on Agoda. I already had a pre-selection on my phone and decided on the P.U. Inn Resort as it was good value for money and had a good location.

When she came back from the bathroom, the mood suddenly changed. Ao hardly said a word, she was very serious. When I asked her something, she answered with a matter-of-factness and distance that almost scared me. There was no more kissing or hugging, just a subdued and serious mood.

When we said goodbye, it was as if we were two strangers. A reluctant kiss on the cheek and she was gone without looking in her handbag.

I sat in the room, taking in the silence. The bed was still rumpled, her scent still surrounded me. I felt a melancholy, like after the end of a long relationship. There was an endless desolation inside me and I wanted to run after her. Finally I made up my mind, packed my things and checked out.

I took the BTS from Nana to Victory Monument, where the minibuses depart. I didn't even bother to look because every station looked the same to me and I didn't feel like walking around in circles three times. I asked immediately and was sent straight to the right direction. I bought a ticket at the counter and while I waited for the bus, I stayed in the ticket seller's line of sight.

I've got into the habit of doing this so they can alert me if I don't realise that my bus is there.

Then it finally pulled up, and a few moments later I was sitting in a single seat on the well cooled minibus.

I was well aware that minibuses are not the least dangerous way to travel. But in this case I chose it because it was quick and easy. Besides, the minibus station in Ayutthaya was very close to my hotel.

Victory Monument

In the early afternoon I entered my hotel room, which I had got for a more than reasonable price. But Ayutthaya is not Bangkok. I didn't unpack my things, and after a quick shower I set off to explore the area.

I walked aimlessly around the area and came to a market just a few hundred metres from the hotel. There I ate some meat skewers with rice and drank some water. I felt very comfortable here, the locals were very attentive and polite, people smiled at me on the street.

I found a tuk-tuk and arranged a little tour with the driver. He was extremely nice, made some sugges-tions about places of interest and offered me the tour for 200 baht an hour. I gratefully accepted and off we went.

My aim was to see the most important temples outside the river ring. The next day I wanted to explore the temples inside the ring on foot.

Actually, most of the temples were ruins and no longer used for prayer. Even though there were often only remnants left, I still found it worthwhile to see them all. I got a good idea of what an impressive empire Ayutthaya must have been before the Burmese army invaded and practically razed the city to the ground.

Wat Chai Watthanaram

I found Wat Chai Watthanaram, a Unesco World Heritage Site, very impressive. The way the Buddha was enthroned in front of the Prang was a great sight. I took my time at this temple and absorbed the atmosphere. I was taken by the spirit that these ancient walls had.

But I was most impressed by Wat Phanan Choeng, where the ceremonies were taking place.

The temple was pretty busy, it was full of tourists arriving by buses. When I saw the huge golden Buddha, I could understand it.

I mingled with the people and bought a folded orange cloth that was handed to me on a tray. Like the others, I added some notes and waited for the assistants to take the cloth with the notes from me.

Wat Phanan Choeng

Then they knotted the cloths, which were huge, and put them around the Buddha as a cloak. A mystical tension gripped the people, which also spread to me.

The lower part of the cloak was draped over us, so that for a moment we sat protectively under the Buddha's cloak. At the end of the ceremony, the cloak was pulled away with a jerk.

It was early evening when I returned to the hotel. I set off to see the area and walked into the centre, if there was such a thing as a centre. I could forget that there was any nightlife, but I knew that beforehand. At best there were some karaoke bars, but tourists hardly ever went there.

I did some shopping before I went back to the hotel. In the evening I sat down at the "Street Lamp Bar & Restaurant", just a few metres from the P.U. Inn Resort. A live band was playing, and it was creating a great atmosphere. Rock songs blasted through the street. The music matched the rustic ambience of the bar. I ate a delicious Thai dish, drank a few beers and enjoyed the good atmosphere.

As far as the ladies were concerned, nothing happened here. The staff were pretty nice and one of them even flirted with me, but I was aware of the limits.

I wondered how many messages I already had on line. Ao must have bombarded me again. I looked at my mobile and ... nothing.

Nothing at all.

I checked to see if I had an online connection at all, but everything was fine. I sent a test message to myself, which arrived a few seconds later, leaving me staring at my phone, a little perplexed.

She was somehow different in the morning, I'd noticed that of course, but I couldn't interpret what it was. Maybe she was expecting me to take her with me. Maybe she was just resigned, because she had hoped for something I couldn't give her. I didn't have the slightest idea what her experiences with other men had been like.

Street Lamp Bar & Restaurant

I thought about what I might have done wrong. Had I perhaps said or done something to offend her? But for the life of me I had no idea of anything that could have gone wrong.

I wondered where Ao was and what she was doing. Was she in Roi Et or still in Bangkok? Maybe in the go-go bar, dancing on the pole. I had images of her standing half-naked in the spotlight, being ogled greedily by the men. Maybe she was sitting with someone, her hand down his trousers, her tongue down his throat. The thought gave me a deep cut in my heart.

Was it the famous love disease?

Love disease is often talked about in Thailand in a very derisive way. A lot of people sneer at it, although most people know that it occurs to everyone sooner or later. And if you travel to Thailand regularly, it will affect you at some point, whether you want it to or not.

It goes far beyond the typical infatuation and can leave men wanting. It is an unending urge to be with a woman... a Thai woman. You can get your heart broken anywhere in the world, but the love disease is not just a broken heart. It's the hammer blow that feels like the skin is being torn from your body.

I wasn't quite there yet, but I was obviously on a good path.

But why does this feeling cause men such endless agony that they can no longer think clearly and are willing to do anything for their Thai beauty?

Usually what happens is that you meet a woman, you get to know her and you develop feelings. You fall in love and it feels good. Then you decide to stay together and have a relationship, which usually has a rational basis. It's not a mindless infatuation that takes over your mind, it's more a mixture of palpitations and horniness. When this relationship breaks down, you feel bad. A big part of this is the ego, or wounded vanity, which can be seen in the fact that it is hard to bear the idea that she could be in bed with someone else right now.

In Thailand, however, this heartbreak is compounded by a serious criterion. Most men who come to Thailand and are single have had failed relationships or are divorced; some have never had a real relationship. Some have long since put women out of their minds and come to terms with it. When such a man - like me - goes to Thailand and meets a beautiful Thai woman who reads all his wishes from his eyes, fulfils all his forgotten dreams in bed and sends him into an emotional firework display... then something happens...

What happens then is much more than infatuation, it comes from the depths of the subconscious. It is something that has always been there, but it has been buried, repressed or forgotten.

When these things come up in you, they amplify the infatuation immeasurably.

I would argue that most people in our society, apart from psychologists, do not know this or cannot even begin to understand it.

These feelings that then arise turn the most rational person into an emotional nervous wreck. They cannot think, they cannot sleep, and some are unable to socialise when they return home.

More than a few men have lost their homes and farms because they sold everything they had and sent the money to Thailand.

Even though the term 'love disease' is mostly used with a wink, it makes sense to see it as a real disease.

How do you protect yourself from love disease?

Quite simply ... not at all.

If you think you are immune or smarter, you have already lost. Then you are walking around as an emotional block and you don't have much fun, or it hits you when you least expect it.

The best remedy for this disease is awareness. Awareness that everyone in Thailand can get it and will get it sooner or later. It doesn't stop the pain, but it keeps the mind working. That's why I keep listening to myself and admitting that something might be coming.

Many men try to protect themselves by avoiding being with a woman for more than three days. I have this rule in my mind too, but I have broken it many times.

Of course, not every relationship with a Thai woman ends in disaster. There are many examples where men are happily married. But you have to be aware that it can be very expensive, depending on background, family situation and expectations.

You also have to be culturally open-minded. If you cannot accept the Thai culture and idiosyncrasies, you will have a hard time.

Where the journey leads in the end is something everyone has to decide for themselves.

The music was off, the bar had drained. Lively conversation echoed around the room from the staff as they cleared the tables.

I checked my mobile again, still no messages.

I checked Badoo and Tinder. The number of girls in the area was much lower than in Bangkok, but there were some. There were some really pretty girls, so I wisely gave them a few likes, paid my bill and went to bed early.

8

On this day, temple exploration was the order of the day - what else in Ayutthaya? First, I took it easy with a simple but good breakfast at the hotel.

I couldn't help checking my mobile phone, but there were no messages that day either. Now I sent Ao a waving sticker, asked if everything was OK and how she was doing. After that, a few more likes on Badoo and Tinder, and I was ready for the temple tour.

For the first few temples I took a tuk-tuk again because of the distances. I had approached a driver on the street and explained what I had already seen and what I still wanted to see. He was extremely friendly and made the same offer as his colleague the day before, which seemed to be the standard price.

I started with Wat Phu Khao Thong, a mix of Burmese and Thai architectural styles. The temple could be seen from a distance, standing imposingly in the landscape. I climbed the stairs, which was pretty sweaty in the heat. When I reached the top, I was rewarded with a great view.

Wat Phu Khao Thong

I continued on to Wat Yai Chaimongkol where there was a lot going on. Apparently this was one of the most popular temples. There were many tourist groups arriving by bus. But there was a lot to see here too. Sitting Buddhas in long rows, a large reclining Buddha and an impressive Chedi.

It was also possible to climb up to this temple, but the view was not as good as at Wat Phu Khao Thong.

When I got back to the tuk-tuk, I found that the whole car park was full of tuk-tuks. Unfortunately, I had forgotten what the tuk-tuk looked like and couldn't really remember the driver. Usually drivers pay attention to you, but I remembered that he wanted to wait for me somewhere else, but where? Annoyed, I looked around for about 20 minutes until I saw him waving. He hadn't expected me so early and had gone to get something to eat. I usually take a picture of the vehicle and number plate on every tour, but this time I had forgotten.

Wat Yai Chaimongkol

I explored a few more temples that were outside, but there was nothing to blow me away. So I got off at Wat Lokayasutharam to explore the rest on foot.

At this temple there was really nothing else except a huge reclining Buddha.

When I went to have a closer look at the Buddha, an elderly lady stopped me. She wanted me to perform a ritual. For a few baht she gave me a candle to light, flowers and a medal. We went together to the Buddha and she instructed me to bow, then place the flowers and light the candle. I was allowed to keep the medallion with the image of Buddha on it. Although it was from the mass press, I had put it in my pocket and kept it as a talisman. I thanked the lady kindly and looked around.

Wat Lokayasutharam

You often see this in old temples in Thailand, but also in Cambodia or Laos, that older people are there. They usually have these lucky ribbons that they tie around you in a ritual way. I almost always go along with that because I think it's a good thing. The old people are not as well provided for as they are in Germany. The pension is ridiculous and they can't live on it if they haven't saved anything ... and who has? Usually the family takes care of the elderly, but unfortunately not everyone has a family and they are left to fend for themselves. They are too proud to beg, so some go that way, sit in the temples and do the rituals with the tourists.

I walked all over the inner ring of the river. I could have rented a bike, which would have been much more efficient, but I wanted to walk so I didn't mind wandering around. There were lots of temples to explore, I looked at everything, but by now I was pretty overloaded with all the impressions and information. I found it hard to follow everything. Sometimes I didn't even know where I was coming from or which direction I was actually going. Sometimes I stood in front of a temple and wondered if I hadn't been there before.

It was different at Wat Thammikarat, which still serves the faithful for praying and celebrating.

With a little excitement I arrived at the most famous temple in Ayutthaya, Wat Mahathat, where the famous buddha head was in a fig tree. When I entered the temple complex, I didn't have to look far, just went to where most of the people were milling about.

Wat Thammikarat

The story goes that the Buddhists buried the head to protect it when the Burmese army attacked the city. Over the years, the roots of the fig tree brought the head to light, where it can be admired today.

Wat Mahathat

Then I went back to the market, got some fruit from a stall and sat down at a nearby table. It was a bit uncomfortable, but the atmosphere was worth it. The people were friendly and relaxed, always smiling. The scent of spices I didn't recognise tickled my nose. The babble of voices in a language I knew a bit of, but in the end barely understood.

I looked at my mobile phone, where there was still no message, but that didn't bother me any more. It was time to accept that Ao would remain a beautiful memory. I realised that this was the best thing that could have happened to me. A clean exit with a nice memory saves a lot of grief.

Street Scene

Then I saw a message on WeChat. I didn't even have that app on my radar. A lady from my neighbourhood was sending me a greeting and wanted to add me as a friend. I accepted, said hello back and looked at the pictures she had posted. She had taken a few selfies and was looking quite nice. I estimated her age to be mid-30s, with a few curves, but generally slim. The face seemed friendly, she smiled discreetly, had warm eyes. I was not surprised to find out that she was a massage lady. I wouldn't have reacted that way in Bangkok, but there wasn't much going on here apart from sightseeing, so it was time for a relaxing massage.

She responded quickly and asked me a few questions about how long I would be staying, how old I was and if I liked massages. Then I started asking questions and wanted to know what kind of massages she offered. She said it depended on me, which left some room for my imagination. I wanted to know if she would like to come to my hotel, I could use a massage. She didn't respond at first and then asked for a recent photo of me. I sent her one immediately and a few seconds later we had an appointment for 7pm at my hotel. When I gave her the name of the hotel, no further description was necessary. She sent a sticker with a thumb up and wrote that we would see each other later.

I first had to come to my senses and realise what I had done again. Actually I only wanted to have a snack and now I had an appointment for a massage, where I hadn't clarified exactly what kind of massage and, above all, how much it would cost.

Now I was really excited, thinking about whether I should tidy up the room or whether there was something I should hide. Then I remembered that I wasn't sure at all about the Hotel Joiner-Fee. On the other hand, she wasn't going to spend the night with me, just give me a massage... and maybe a hand job.

I quickly walked to the hotel and checked the room. Nothing embarrassing was lying around, the dirty laundry was in the suitcase. Apart from that, the maid had made everything spotless. I showered, shaved and selected some relaxing music on my iPad. Then I passed the time looking at her photos on mobile phone.

Just after 7pm there was a knock on my door, I opened it and there she was. I had to look down quite far, she was probably not 1.50m tall. Slightly uncertain, almost shy, she looked at me. I smiled, let her in and offered her something to drink. We drank water and talked. She wanted to know how I had spent my holiday, what I had already seen and what I still wanted to see. She told me about herself without giving away too much personal information. Then we got down to business. She wanted 300 baht for an oil massage, which I thought was OK. She got some utensils from her bag while I undressed completely and lay down on the bed.

Lying on my stomach, I heard her open the bottle of oil and soon her hands were stroking my back. I knew immediately that she was something special. She skilfully felt all the tension in my body and massaged it out without me feeling much pain. From my back she went up to my shoulders and from there to my arms. Then she started massaging my feet and calves, from where her hands worked their way up my legs.

As she slid up the inside of my thighs, I felt something stir. Almost accidentally, she touched the swelling that had formed between my legs for a brief moment, causing a slight lack of space beneath me.

Now it was time to turn around. I did so and lay there with a full mast. A little embarrassed, although that was actually nothing unusual. With a discreet and knowing smile, she overlooked my arousal and acted as if nothing was wrong. Now she massaged my upper body, continuing on my stomach and almost inadvertently touching my cock, which now didn't even think about relaxing.

Her hands slid around it until she had mercy and took it in her hand. Now it was time to negotiate the price, with me in the worst possible position. It would have been wiser to discuss it beforehand, but I found the uncertainty exciting. But once again there was an honest woman who offered me a handjob for 500 baht more, a really fair price.

She laid out some cloths, took a large amount of oil and massaged my best part with her fingertips. The slippery feeling of the oil made me infinitely hot. Then she enclosed my cock with her hand and jerked me off at a moderate pace. She took her time, confident that she would get me there anyway. With her other hand she caressed my balls and gently squeezed my prostrate shaft.

It tingled more and more and I felt that it would soon be time. Satisfied, with a quiet smile, she continued without hurrying. She varied her movements, sometimes slowing down and stroking just a little, only to drive me crazy with faster hand movements. I could hardly stand it any longer and grabbed her breasts. She lifted her t-shirt and let me knead her breast.

Finally it came out of me in violent spurts. I was dizzy with excitement, I felt it more intensely than during sex. After I had filled my belly, she slowed down her movements, squeezing a little to get it all out. It seemed she had enjoyed herself, she was still smiling her soft smile and seemed satisfied.

Without rushing, she cleaned me up and handed me a glass of water before disappearing into the bathroom.

Half an hour later I was still sitting there, grinning, happy about this little massage adventure that had been more than worth it.

Then I went to the same restaurant as the night before and planned my onward journey to Kanchanaburi.

9

After breakfast I checked out and walked to the minibus station which was only a few minutes walk away. There was no direct bus to Kanchanaburi, I had to change at Suphanburi.

It didn't take long and the bus was full and on its way. I was grateful to have caught a sensible driver again. Unfortunately, Thailand is a very dangerous country when it comes to road traffic, with one of the highest death rates in the world. There are various causes for this, from carelessness to alcohol to driving without a licence. Carelessness is most prevalent among minibus drivers, some of whom drive like mad. As a result, there are often serious accidents, which makes this mode of transport one of the riskiest. I was all the more grateful for the careful driving of this driver.

After about half an hour, the bus pulled to the right and the driver was talking to the passenger. I could see that a warning light was on in the driver's cockpit.

Then it was time to get out. We followed the instructions, stood at the side of the road and watched the driver helplessly look under the bonnet.

I wondered why he didn't reach for his mobile phone and organise a replacement bus. Somehow he was convinced it would still work.

Twenty minutes later we were back in the bus. When he started the engine, the warning was still there. He drove on anyway, but at a much reduced speed. All the consumers were now switched off. From the car radio to the ventilation to the ... air conditioning. In order not to die of heat stroke, fout side windows were opened, which were as efficient as Don Quixote against the windmills. But I was happier sitting by one of the open windows.

Finally we arrived at the bus station in Suphanburi. I didn't have to worry about anything. Someone immediately came up to me and asked where I was going. I told him and he manoeuvred me to another staff member who took me and pushed me towards another colleague who put me on a local bus. I sat in the last row because the luggage was stacked in front of me and I could see my suitcase.

Unfortunately, there was no air conditioning, but fans on the ceiling fought a hopeless battle against the heat. But as the bus set off, a breeze came into the bus. All the side windows were open and together with the fans it was bearable, except for the moments when the bus was stationary.

Local Bus

In Kanchanaburi I took a tuk-tuk to the Good Times Resort, a hotel right on the river. It was quite a distance from the famous bridge, but there were a few bars nearby.

Check-in was quick and easy. At the reception I booked another tour for the next day. Now I had enough time for a walk to the famous Bridge on the River Kwai.

I followed the road that ran parallel with the river to the bridge. As I had expected, there were a lot of tourists at the bridge. This sight was the main attraction in Kanchanaburi, so it was very busy.

As I was about to cross, I was surprised to see a train arriving. This bridge was actually still in use. It was full of people and the train was approaching at walking speed. There was no great danger, however, as there were plenty of places on the sides for people to get out of the way. But it was a strange sight, unlike anything I had ever seen in Germany.

Bridge on the RiverKwai

When the train had passed, I went over to look at the temple on the other side. To my surprise, there was nothing going on at all. Not even a handful of tourists were there. It was a Chinese temple and an oasis of calm compared to the hustle and bustle on the other side of the river. It was getting dark and I strolled back across the now empty bridge to the ho-tel.

Chinese Temple - Bridge on the River Kwai

In the evening I went to a club near the hotel, which I had discovered by chance. It was a bar and restaurant with live music. The name was โกดังเสือดี and it was pronounced Goa Dang Süa Dii, which means House of the Good Tiger.

The club was a kind of loft with big wooden tables lined up side by side. There was a stage at the front and a bar at the back. A staircase led up to a gallery where you could play billiards.

As I stepped inside, the bass line of the rock song the band was playing ran through me. It was quite crowded, but I was lucky enough to find a seat near the bar. At a table next to me was a group of young men who were partying. Everyone here was in a party mood, the alcohol was flowing, the atmosphere was boisterous. I was astonished to see that I was the only tourist in the place. I ordered some food and a beer and enjoyed the band which gave a great performance.

The partying men made friendly toasts to me, drinking and laughing boisterously. From time to time a friendly word was exchanged and by the time I had spoken a few words of Thai, I was their buddy. Like many Thais, they were very curious and wanted to know where I was from and how often I visited Thailand. It was quite nice, but also exhausting to talk against the loud music.

They told me about the confusion of names at the Bridge on the River Kwai.

Because of the film "The Bridge on the River Kwai", it was assumed that the Kwai River flowed there. But Kwai means river, and the Kwai itself was somewhere else. Pragmatic as they are, the Thais simply renamed the river the Kwai River and the problem was solved.

There was another misunderstanding with the word buffalo, which is also spelt Kwai in the Phonetic language. It is a different kwai, however, and is pronounced quite differently. But nobody who doesn't know the Thai alphabet could know that. So tourists asked where the buffaloes were, thinking the bridge was named after buffaloes.

Bar & Restaurant

The story amused me, but it also made me realise how quickly confusion can arise when you learn Thai without studying the script and pronunciation.

I remembered that I once made a mistake myself when I wanted to tell a lady that I thought she was pretty. The word Süai means pretty and mispronounced it means someone who brings bad things.

The evening was nearing its climax and the alcohol was taking its effect. The guys were completely drunk, which was the sign for me to leave.

Thais are lovely and nice people, but when they are drunk you should see that you get away. Unfortunately, the cliché that many Asians can't hold their liquor is true. Somehow their bodies can't process alcohol as well, which makes it much harder for them to get drunk than for people in our latitudes.

Unfortunately, this means that Thais often go mad when they are drunk and do things they would never do when sober. Many accidents in Thailand happen when people are drunk, just look at the accident statistics. Fights can also break out quickly. It is particularly explosive when a joke is misunderstood and the issue of losing face comes into play. Loss of face and alcohol are a dangerous mix and can end terribly. Such situations are often not apparent. The mood can change from one second to the next, even though we were getting along fine just a moment before.

I told the guys that I had had enough to drink and wanted to get up early the next day. After a warm and friendly goodbye, I went back to the hotel.

When I was in the room, I had a message from Ao. She wrote "Hi" in reply to my message. It didn't look like a storm of enthusiasm, but on the other hand she didn't ignore me either. I wondered what was wrong with her and what I had done wrong. I could have just asked her, but I knew she wouldn't answer me. Thai women don't talk about problems, they keep quiet and sit it out.

I had to ask myself one question. Why am I worrying so much about a woman I hardly know? A woman with whom I have nothing in common except good sex and a little care.

I had heard so many stories about love disease, had experienced it myself... but it had never happened that I couldn't get a woman out of my mind after such a short time.

I decided not to write her back and went to bed brooding.

10

The first stop of the day was the Erawan Waterfall. When we arrived there, I was glad to have put on my good sports shoes. The waterfall stretched over seven steps, some of which had to be climbed over boulders that were difficult to climb. The first steps were no problem, but the higher I got, the more challenging it became. No athletic skills were required, but some of the rocks were pretty slippery. Slipping on them would certainly not be pleasant. It wasn't particularly high, but there were hard, angular stones where you could easily break a few bones. However, with my sports shoes I was able to walk over the rocks easily.

The struggle to get there was definitely worth it. I felt like I was in paradise. It was a turquoise oasis in the middle of the jungle. People were bathing on some levels, for which the waterfall was wonderful. The top level was the busiest. If you made it to the top, you didn't want to leave in a hurry.

Erawan waterfall

Then we went to the wooden bridge, which impressed me a lot. A wooden bridge in the middle of the idyll. You could be thrilled by this beautiful place and the great view of Thailand's wonderful nature. But the atmosphere there was also gloomy. There is a sad story behind the construction of this bridge.

It is also known as the Railway of Death, which is not an exaggeration. The Japanese built the railway during the Second World War to create a connection with Myanmar. The railway line was built mainly by prisoners of war, but also by Thais condemned to forced labour. The enemy was not supposed to know that the line was being built, so everything had to be done in secret. Therefore, there was no heavy equipment available, as is usually the case, instead everything was built by hand. When looking at the wooden bridge, it is hard to believe how it could be done by hand, but it was done... at a high price.

People had to work twenty hours a day without proper food or drink. If someone became sick, it was a death sentence; if someone collapsed under the strain, the same thing happened.

Wooden Bridge

Later we continued with the train that still officially runs there. To get a little Thai feeling, we sat in third class. The locals were not so stupid and sat in second class.

Then I went back to the Bridge on the River Kwai, where I had already been the day before. I said

110

goodbye in a friendly manner, gave the nice guide a good tip and visited the museum. Practically everything related to the construction of the railway was displayed here. Many fates, many numbers that I couldn't remember in the end, but shocking in detail.

From the terrace of the museum, the view was magnificent. I lingered there for a while, took a few photos and then made my way back.

Bridge on the River Kwai from the Museum

On the way there was a Thai restaurant where I had a bite to eat before I wanted to find a nice bar in the evening. Today I was in the mood for a girl bar.

I walked back to the main road that was leading parallel to the river, but now in the opposite direction.

It didn't take long and I could see the lights of a few bars and restaurants. There weren't many shops here, but for a nice evening it was okay.

A few girls called out to me from a bar and waved. The rustic and colourfully lit ambience made a pleasant impression, the girls were pretty, so I went in.

I was immediately taken over by a cute girl who hooked herself up with me and led me to a table. She was very cheerful and had a lot of funny things to say. When we were seated, I ordered drinks for both of us, which won me some points with the ladyboy behind the bar. We made ourselves comfortable and while she was introducing herself, she put her hand on my balls. The girl was naughty as hell, chatting openly about size and hardness while she rubbed her hand between my legs. When our drinks came we toasted and kissed.

Her name was Pim, she was 26 years old and lived in the area. A short black dress adorned her slender body. The dress had a zip at the front, which I would have loved to open at the sight of her cleavage. The beginnings of her breasts were clearly visible and aroused my imagination.

It didn't take long before another girl appeared behind us. Nut was the name of the girl who was sneaking up on me from the other side. She saw Pim's hand between my legs and added hers. Pim screamed in horror and asked how she could put her hand on my balls, they belonged to her. Nut replied that it was her right to have them too. So the whole thing escalated into an artificial argument, accompanied by a lot of cackling. Some of the package tourists in the bar looked away in embarrassment.

I calmed the two squabblers down by ordering a couple of drinks for us, which worked well. Now they were fumbling together between my legs, rubbing and groping, discussing size and stamina.

At some point I shouted, "Hey girls, I hear you.

They laughed and didn't care at all. They just wanted to have fun and do their thing, which was exactly what I needed to do that night.

I was the centre of attention all the time, kissing one side, kissing the other, groping, laughing and having a great time.

Some time later they started discussing which one of them would accompany me to the hotel, whereupon another artificial argument broke out. It was clear to me that it would be Pim, she was just so sweet. Now I had to communicate my decision without making Nut loose her face. Luckily in this case it was easy. I said first come, first paint, and that was accepted. Pim was happy with my decision and thanked me with an extra stroke between my legs and a wet kiss. I asked about the conditions and she told me 1000 baht for a short time. I was stunned by the price, which I found almost unpleasantly low for such a nice girl.

The ladyboy brought the bill, which also listed the 300 baht barfine I had to pay for Pim's loss of work. Now it was Nut's turn to entertain the guests and sell drinks.

We rode on her moped to my hotel, which I didn't really understand given the short distance. But for Thai girls, everything over 200 metres is a marathon.

In the room we took a shower together, where she devotedly soaped me up. Finally I could see her as I had imagined her all along and I was not disappointed. I also took some shower gel and soaped up her body. In between we kissed, which drove me crazy.

Bar in Kanchanaburi

We moved to the bed and cuddled. She was not shy, had not tied a towel around her or pulled a blanket over her. We caressed each other's bodies without haste. Then she took the initiative and kissed my chest. She worked her way down and pampered me with her mouth. I looked down at her and enjoyed the feeling she was giving me with her lips and tongue.

Then she crawled back up, kissed me and put a rubber on me that was on the bedside table. She sat on me and started to ride. At first she varied the speed until she increased it. Our pelvises hit each other faster and faster until it almost hurt. She rode me like a percussion drill, moaning loudly as I kneaded her breasts with my hands.

After a while the pace became too intense for me and we switched to Missy where I took it slower. She was panting and pinning me down with her feet, thrusting her pelvis against me with every thrust.

Deeply relieved, I finally came and happily dropped down on my side next to her.

We chatted for a while before she left with 1500 baht in her handbag.

I had another beer in my room and checked Agoda for hotels in Bangkok. This time I chose the Admiral Premier Inn in Soi 23. It was behind Soi Cowboy, so I had to walk a bit, but the price was much better than at the Phachara Suites. The rooms at the Admiral were a bit shabbier, but for the price they were perfectly acceptable.

Just to be on the safe side, I checked online to see if the hotel really did not take a joiner's fee, which would have been annoying.

There are some hotels that do not accept girls as guests, and if they do, then only for a hefty fee that can quickly add up to 1000 or 2000 baht. There are a lot of websites now that provide information about hotels that don't charge for girls, and more are being added all the time. On a search engine, I always find what I'm looking for quickly using the combination of hotel + Thailand + girlfriend/bargirlfriendly.

After researching, the hotel turned out to be okay and I booked for my last two nights.

11

I took my time at breakfast and enjoyed the beautiful view of the river. I felt very comfortable in the hotel and was sure to come back.

Afterwards I took a tuk-tuk to the minibus.

View at the Good Times Resort

The drive to Bangkok was relaxed. The driver was okay, the air conditioning worked and the car didn't make any fuss.

Arriving at the Victory Monument, I took the BTS Skytrain to Asoke station, from where I walked another ten minutes to the hotel.

For most people, Bangkok stops at Soi Cowboy, which is a pity. There are some really good cafes and restaurants behind it. In the Soi Cowboy area, there are a few massage parlours on Soi 23 that leave nothing to be desired. However, as soon as you turn off, the offer changes according to the crowd. One massage shop has a big sign saying "No Sex". There is no nightlife, except for a club. However, it is definitely recommendable to go out for a meal or a coffee.

As it was early afternoon, I decided to go exploring. I got on the BTS and this time I didn't go in the direction of Siam, instead I went in the opposite direction to Samrong station. There was no particular reason for me to go there, it was a spontaneous decision.

I have made it a habit to go to places in Bangkok that I know nothing about. I like to give in to the impressions and let myself be surprised. I don't expect any special sights or highlights. I want to see Bangkok as it is, away from the tourist crowds.

I walked back across the river and turned right because the map on my phone showed a temple there. The path led along a busy shopping street with small shops, tuk-tuks, cookshops and - not to be missed - Seven Eleven stores.

These shops can be found all over the country and are a reliable constant around the clock. You can rely on the wide range of products on offer and the well-run air-conditioning systems to keep you cool in the tropical heat.

Samrong – Road to the temple

You can even call the tourist police at Seven Eleven shops if you are in trouble. It is recommended that you do not go to the local police if you have a problem, but to the tourist police if possible.

I didn't have to go far and I was heading right for Wat Dan Samrong. The temple was not very big, but nice to look at.

I walked around a bit, watching the relaxed monks gardening, chatting or just sitting around, and then I walked back.

Wat Dan Samrong

My next destination was Imperial World Samrong, which I could already see from the BTS. The mall was of impressive size, generally the malls in Thailand are always quite large. There were no tourists to be seen, the occasional expat crossed my path, but that was about it. The mall was no different from most, with the usual shops for general needs. I walked from floor to floor, enjoying the pleasant coolness and noticing that people were paying more attention to me here than in the Siam area.

On the top floor there were some small shops run by private individuals which were very interesting. I ended up in a CD shop and was thrilled. He didn't have a huge selection, but he had hidden away some jewels of Thai pop music that were no longer available in the usual CD shops.

After buying two CDs, I had a coffee and looked at the people. When a group of young women walked by, I couldn't help thinking of Ao and wondering what she was doing. Was she at home in Roi Et or was she back in Bangkok working in a go-go bar?

Puzzled, I decided it was better not to think about it and drove back to the hotel.

My first port of call in the evening was the Old German Beerhouse on Soi 11.

I ordered a Thai curry, which was my favourite thing to eat there. There was also a large selection of traditional German dishes, which were very good, but I liked the Thai curry best. While I polished off the food and drank freshly tapped beer, I watched a football match on one of the big monitors. This place invited me to stay and feel good. The interior was modern, clean and the staff friendly. There was another Beerhouse on Soi 13 that looked the same but didn't have the same atmosphere.

After dinner I walked down Sukhumvit Road to Soi 4 where I turned down to Nana Plaza. Without giving it much thought, I went inside and walked down the corridors. As I passed the bar where I met Ao, I peered inside but couldn't see anything. The curtain was only open a tiny crack, barely giving me a glimpse.

After another round, I stood in front of it again and went in with a quick decision. I sat down in the same place as last time and ordered a beer. The Mamasan recognised me and greeted me warmly. I looked around and then it hit me like a punch in the face. Ao was sitting next to a man, laughing, amused, with his hand on his thigh. They were talking animatedly, then kissing here, kissing there, and I could have thrown up. The bitch wasn't in Roi Et and hadn't stopped at the go-go bar. She did something else and cheekily lied to me.

A girl wanted to sit with me, but I sent her away without paying attention to her.

I saw Ao looking at the guy and it hit me hard. I felt so desperate at that moment and had no idea why. She wasn't my girlfriend or my partner. She wasn't even an affair. It was just a business relationship for a period of time, nothing more. I tried to think rationally and calm down, but it was damn hard, I was too shocked.

Now she put her arms around his neck and kissed him, rubbing her hand between his legs. I looked elsewhere, but my eyes kept going back to her.

Then she looked over and recognised me immediately. She twitched briefly and looked at me in confusion. Obviously she hadn't expected me.

Ao got a sign that it was her turn to dance, stood on the stage and began to move lethargically. From time to time she smiled at the guy, but she didn't even look at me. She ignored me completely, as if I were a stranger.

I paid for the beer and hurried out. I walked aimlessly around the area, trying to clean up the pile of broken pieces inside me.

As rationally as I could, I began to explain the situation and my emotional chaos to myself. She was a go-go girl, I was a customer. She was with me because there was money, but I had a girlfriend by my side - for a while. We parted ways when I moved on. For me, a few more days of holiday were in order, and then the journey home, where a well-paid job was waiting for me. For Ao, nothing was waiting except the alternativelessness of the go-go bar. I came to the conclusion that it would be unfair to blame her and gradually calmed down.

Now the question was how best to get rid of the heartache, just at the moment when I passed Soi 7/1.

I went to the Wood, which was known as a blowjob bar. I walked in with determination and was greeted in a very friendly way by the Mamasan. She asked me if I had been there before and I honestly said no. She briefly explained the procedure and the cost - 1000 baht - and then had the girls line up.

I chose an unassuming but cute mouse who looked like a student. With her thick glasses, she looked like a nerd. Combined with the super-short checked skirt and white blouse, it really turned me on. It was quick and easy. I followed her down a corridor into a room not much bigger than a massage parlour. There was a sink in the room and some sort of armchair. I undressed, she washed me at the sink and then asked me to sit in the chair. When I was seated, she moved the back of the chair slightly backwards to make it more comfortable. Then she took a thick cushion and placed it in front of me, and then knelt on it.

The mouse took my cock directly into her mouth without any preliminaries. I noticed immediately that extraordinary skills were at work here, within seconds the thing was standing like a one. She gave me the most varied blowjob I had ever experienced. She took it deep into her mouth, turning her head and occasionally pressing her lips together. She paused in between, licked my glans and balls with her tongue and finally took it deep into her mouth again.

Careful not to come too soon, she kept stopping for a few moments to play with her tongue, only to bring me closer again. She repeated the game a couple of times until I finally came in her mouth with greater ease.

We talked for quite a while, and she asked me some personal questions, like you do when you meet someone for the first time. She had an incredibly likeable charisma and was somehow my type. If she hadn't worked in a bar like that, she would have been something for me. But that bar would give me too much of a headache if I kissed her.

Happily, I left the shop, not without leaving the mouse a good tip.

On Sukhumvit Road, I sat down at Margarita Storm and had a few beers outside while watching the hustle and bustle on the street.

Of course, I couldn't get Ao out of my mind. The images were playing in my mind all the time, without me being able to do anything about it, without me being able to distract myself. I had to admit that I was already beginning to like her.

Sukhumvit Road

I allowed myself to feel sorry for myself for the rest of the evening and drank until the dizziness set in, which accompanied me all the way to bed.

My last thoughts were that I wanted to forget Ao and never see her again. The whole situation was too delicate and I was being unreasonable.

Then I fell asleep.

12

In the morning I took the metro from Asoke station to Hua Lamphong, China Town. The Metro works the same way as the BTS Skytrain. You choose the station at the vending machine, make your change and get your ticket. Unfortunately the Rabbit Card only works on the BTS, but luckily the vending machine was not very busy, so it was quick.

From Hua Lamphong station I walked to the railway station to have a look inside. Outside I was approached by touts trying to lead me to travel agencies. I told them I just wanted to look around and went inside. Inside I saw the ticket office, where you can get tickets cheaper than in one of the travel agencies. I looked around and thought about going by train. Then I left the station and went to my real destination, a temple nearby.

Wat Traimit is the most famous temple in the China Town area. Inside this temple was a large golden Buddha, nothing unusual in itself, but this Buddha was actually made of a high percentage of gold. I wondered if anyone had ever thought of stealing it, but five and a half tonnes is not something you can just put in your pocket.

I went up a flight of stairs and took a few photos from the top, but the skyline was not particularly spectacular. The Buddha, on the other hand, had already impressed me. There were a few tourists here who mingled with the worshippers who were praying there. I went up to a monk and got my next bracelet, then some holy water in a little bottle to take with me.

Wat Traimit

Freshly blessed, I plunged into the crowds of China Town, where I immediately got lost. Without knowing exactly where I was, I walked through the narrow corridors. Densely packed, people pushed their way along without hurrying or jostling. Every now and then a moped would come along, somehow weaving its way through the crowd. One or two food vendors stopped their pushcart in the middle of the path, where there was already too little space.

China Town

The Thais were so incredibly relaxed about these situations. It would have been unimaginable for us.

When I left China Town, I continued to walk around aimlessly. When I realised I had no idea where I was, I looked it up on my mobile phone. My way led me towards Sathan Taksin, which was quite convenient. There was the new Iconsiam Mall on the other side of the river. There was a lot of hype about this mall, so I wanted to see for myself.

I went to the pier where I had already been for the river trip to the Royal Palace. This time I also passed the ticket booths for the blue boats to the end and waited for the free boat shuttle. It didn't take long and after a few minutes I entered the mall.

At the front were shops with brands I couldn't afford, at the back were the shops for the majority of people.

It was all nicely done, but it didn't really blow me away. I wondered if Bangkok really needed this mall. It was like planting a tree in an overgrown forest.

What I really liked, though, were the terraces from which I had a great view over the river.

Away from the shops, the restaurant area in the basement is well worth a visit. There is an endless choice of Asian delicacies. The atmosphere is authentically based on the different regions. Events and performances take place here from time to time.

It is well worth taking a stroll around. This area is also very popular with the local girls.

View from Iconsiam Mall

Before I went back to the hotel, I visited Wat Yannawa , which was only a few metres away from the BTS Station. Someone had the creative idea to build a temple in the shape of a junk.

There was a sort of museum where you could buy souvenirs. But I couldn't help feeling that it was all about money, somehow they wanted to make money out of everything. I didn't worry about it any more and went back to the hotel.

For dinner I went to Baan Khanitha, an upmarket Thai restaurant not far from the hotel on Soi 23. It was my last night and I wanted to treat myself to something nice. I ordered a glass of wine and looked at my mobile phone. There was a message that made me swallow.

Wat Yannawa

Ao had written to me. She wanted to know why I hadn't told her I was coming back to Bangkok.

I replied that I was not expecting her as she said she was going home.

She then asked what I was doing at the go-go bar if I wasn't expecting her.

Checkmate!

I should have known better, these tactical games never work.

I put an end to the hypocrisy and wrote that I wanted to see her, to which she replied that she had to work.

I asked her to come to the restaurant, I would give her the barfine she was due.

I wasn't sure if it would work, but I was lucky. It paid off that I had made friends with the Mamasan, who let Ao go. About twenty minutes later she came whizzing by on a motorbike taxi.

When she saw me, she immediately brightened up and came straight to me. This impetuous and natural way was exactly what I had missed.

She was wearing jeans, in which she had a mega-hot figure, sneakers and... a pullover. I could only wonder how she could wear a pullover in Thailand.

I asked her to recommend a good Thai dish and she ordered for me. The atmosphere was not as relaxed as I would have liked. Our eyes were not as bright as before, our smiles were strained and our movements seemed staged. I decided not to ask any questions that might compromise her in any way and told her a bit about Kanchanaburi and Ayutthaya.

After dinner I asked her if she would like to go to a sky bar with me. It was a nice experience last time and I wanted to do it again. She suggested the Octave Sky Bar at the top of the Marriot Hotel on Sukhumvit Road.

In the taxi we were silent. She held my hand and looked dreamily out of the window. I asked her if she was all right, and she looked at me with a smile and thanked me for seeing her.

At the Skybar we were lucky to get a table, because this time we didn't have a reservation. We sat next to each other and looked at the skyline, which was also quite impressive from this bar. We toasted with the red wine I had ordered.

The mood lightened and she cuddled up to me and confessed that she missed me and thought about me every day.

She described to me how she had felt when we first met. When I walked through the corridors of Nana Plaza, she noticed me immediately. She liked me from the first moment and watched carefully where I went. She wanted me and when I passed her, she decided to catch me. She did and I remember with a smile how determined the little lady was.

I was found.

She showed me pictures of her home and her family. Then she told me that she would like to take me to her home to introduce me to her family.

I said I would be happy to accompany her to Roi Et. But I was not sure about this statement. Of course, I was aware that the whole thing could amount to sponsorship.

Octave-Skybar

Many girls in Thailand are sponsored by their boyfriends from abroad. This means that their boyfriend sends them a few hundred euros every month so that they have money for their family and don't have to work in a bar. Now two things can happen. The girl actually goes home and lives happily ever after on the sponsorship... or she pretends to go home, continues to work in the bar and still gets money sent to her. Some girls even have multiple sponsors and earn a lot of money.

The problem for the love freak is that it's hard to know what you're dealing with. In my experience, your best chances are with girls who are brand new to the business and want to get out as soon as possible, or older women who are just tired and looking for someone to retire with.

We didn't finish the wine and went straight back to the hotel by taxi. During the drive she stroked my thigh, which put me in a great mood. I could hardly wait to lie in bed with her.

When we reached the room, we undressed and went into the shower together. As we soaped ourselves, it was like a release to finally touch her body again. We took our time, caressing each other more than washing. I stroked her breasts, felt her hard nipples under my fingertips and kissed them. Greedily we pushed our tongues into each other as our hands simultaneously landed between our legs. She dropped to her knees and without hesitation took my cock in her mouth. I enjoyed her lips and watched as she worked me. But then I had to stop so as not to finish too soon.

We moved over to the bed and I kissed her greedily all over her body. I pushed down and licked her, holding her legs wide apart. Like last time, she pressed herself against me. When I realised she was coming, I held back this time, stimulating her with my finger as I moved it gently inside her. She moaned even louder than the last time and jerked violently, then relaxed with a deep sigh. I pushed myself up, held her tightly in my arms and we kissed for a long time.

I took a rubber, turned her flat on her stomach and penetrated her pussy from behind. She moaned again, panting and holding herself pleasantly against it again. I kissed her neck as I stroked her with gentle movements.

We switched to the missy, where I accelerated. At that moment I could no longer hold back and came violently inside her as we greedily and wetly pushed our tongues into each other's mouths.

We lay together for a while, then I looked at her and saw tears in her eyes. I lay down close to her, took her in my arms and asked her if everything was all right. After a moment of silence she said that everything was fine and that she was just happy.

So we lay there for a while and then she asked me when I was coming back to Thailand. Like last time, I told her I wanted to go back to Thailand as soon as possible.

She tried to explain why she was crying. Stuttering slightly, she said she was afraid she would never see me again. I was a good guy and there aren't many guys like me.

I promised her we would meet again and we fell asleep arm in arm.

13

When we woke up in the morning, we were all over each other again, knowing it was the last time we would be together.

Then she had to go home, but insisted on accompanying me to the airport later. So we arranged to have dinner together again that evening. I left a generous amount of money in her handbag and again she didn't look.

After a shower it was almost noon. I checked out, left my suitcase at the hotel and went to Siam Station to spend some time in the malls.

This had become a ritual for me on the last day. Without the opportunity to shower, I was able to avoid sweating unnecessarily in the malls.

I walked from Siam Discovery Mall to MBK Centre. Here I passed the time, strolled around, had a coffee, had a manicure and then had another coffee.

As always on the last day, I was overcome by the melancholy that comes with the end of a holiday. I thought about all the experiences I had in such a short time. I thought of Phan from the Thermae, who looked so sexy in her white dress, but also of Chan from the beer garden, with whom I had a great night.

But as soon as my thoughts turned to Ao, my heart pounded without me being able - or willing - to do anything about it. I wondered whether it was all over for me now or whether I would soon forget her. It was impossible for me to judge, anything was possible.

Square in front of Siam Paragon Mall

When it started to get dark I went back to the Siam Malls. I strolled around the square in front of Siam Paragon and spent some time outside by the fountain. The BTS Skytrain's were passing overhead, tourists were taking pictures and some teenagers were chilling out.

I found it hard to get away from this place. On the last day, I often feel like a small child who wants to hold on to every place as if he will never see it again.

I took the BTS to Nana station and walked down Soi 8 to the Via Vai restaurant where I had eaten the first night. I ordered a glass of wine and waited for Ao, who arrived a little late.

Soi 8

This time she was wearing a tight cloth dress that reached just above her knees. She had a scarf over her shoulders to protect her from the cold - about 30°C. She looked sad, but was trying to appear in a good mood. We ordered something to eat and chatted as intimately as I had wished. I was grateful that she made it easy for me. These farewell evenings can sometimes be quite theatrical, which wouldn't make things any easier.

I looked at her, watching her lively eyes as she told me about her dreams. She missed Isaan, wanted to go back as soon as possible and open a small shop as soon as she had saved some money. Her biggest wish was to see me again in her home in Isaan. I could stay with her in the house where she lived alone with her two children. During the time she was in Bangkok, the children were staying with her sister, who also had a daughter. Ao showed me pictures on her mobile phone of her house, her garden and her family, her parents, her children, her sister and some other relatives.

It was time to go. I looked around, tuk-tuks drove by, diagonally opposite the ladies sitting outside the massage parlour typing boredly on their mobile phones. Some tourists seemed to have just arrived, rolling their suitcases behind them and looking around excitedly. I envied them, they still had a whole holiday ahead of them... and for me it was time to go.

I paid the bill, looked into Ao's eyes, who looked at me sadly, then we stood up.

I wanted to go to the BTS Station, but Ao persuaded me to take a taxi. I agreed, I didn't care how I got to the airport.

She stopped a taxi, talked to the driver and slammed the door. The next taxi came and the same thing happened. She finally managed it with the third taxi and we got in.

In the taxi she explained to me that the other taxi drivers did not want to use meters, which would have been expensive. Obviously they saw me with the suitcase and thought I would definitely take a taxi. But they had not reckoned with little Ao's assertiveness.

As we sat in the taxi and the lights of the night passed us by, the mood became rather gloomy. We didn't talk much, just held hands and accepted it.

Skyline by night

At the airport everything went quickly. There was not much of a queue at the check-in as I was quite early. Ao took me to the escalator that would take me to the departure area. The escalator of horror, as it is called, is the worst moment of a holiday. It is the irrevocable end of a time in paradise that is abruptly and inevitably over as soon as you step off that escalator.

When we got there, we hugged each other one last time. Ao said she missed me and would wait for me. Tears welled up on her face, she couldn't hold them back any longer. I had to control myself not to cry too. I took her in my arms once more, kissed her on the cheek and we parted. I stood on the escalator and walked up, watching her walk away bit by bit and realising that the journey was over ... and if some stupid cow on the escalator hadn't stared at me so stupidly, I might have shed a tear too.

Then I was back in the grey.

Airport